"You can do all things
through Christ which
strengthens you",
Blessings,
Vicki Watkins

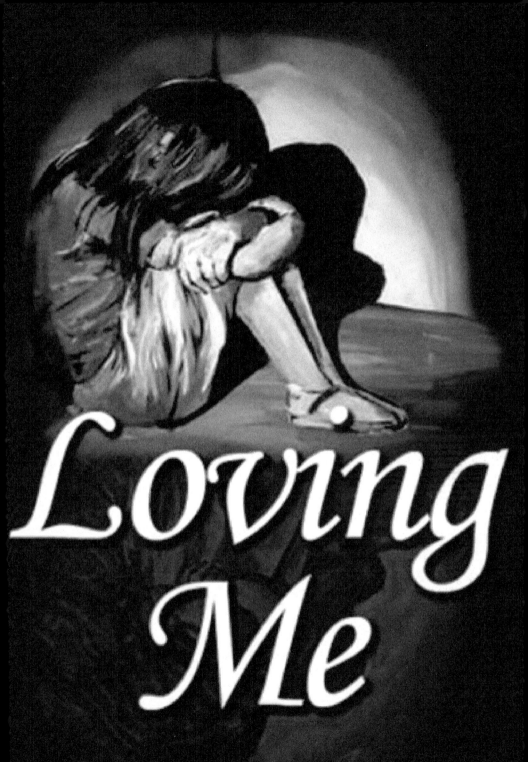

Loving Me

Vicki W. Watkins
John F. Hunt

Outskirts Press, Inc.
http://www.outskirtspress.com

ISBN: 978-1-4787-8068-7

Front Cover Artwork: Jayson Neff

Outskirts Press and the "OP" logo are trademarks belonging to Outskirts Press, Inc.

PRINTED IN THE UNITED STATES OF AMERICA

Dedication

To the healing power of my Lord, Jesus Christ
Letting me know that I am not alone in my journey
And to those who feel alone in their suffering
That they may come to know
The True Healing Power of Jesus Christ

Alfonso Huckleberry Sr.

Loving Me

It's not that I don't love you – I think you know I do

But your tongue is like a knife that leaves my soul to bleed

And leaving you behind is the only way I'll be free

It's not that I don't want to see you or want you to be near

It's just the values I hold precious you don't see are dear

I don't know why we are fighting, we never see eye to eye

When I try to say you've hurt me, you just try to deny

No longer can I struggle and keep the peace

So I guess my saying goodbye is the only way it'll cease

It's not that I won't miss you: I think you now I will

But I must protect my spirit that you are trying hard to kill

It's not an easy thing to do, to turn and run away

But I'm looking towards tomorrow with the hope of a new day

I think I'll be okay now, although it's a long road ahead

I'm going to love myself now and know the abuse is dead

I'll always love you dearly, deep inside my heart

But loving myself now is why we must part

Vicki Watkins, LifeWay 1991

Table of Contents

Foreword

I met Vicki Watkins at our library branch's Local Authors Panel event in November, 2014. She was promoting *Against the Tide,* a book of poetry reflecting on her life's journey and I was promoting *Walking With Jason,* my book on the value of the wilderness to help kids at-risk.

She spoke first and her narrative resonated with me because of my family's involvement with youth at-risk. I listen thinking she could have been one of "our kids." She read her poem "Loving Me" which deepened that feeling. She had used her writing and her finding God to restore herself and move forward in becoming the person she was meant to be.

I spoke last and must have made an impression on Vicki. I spoke of the intrinsic strengths and values children are born with as well as the innate powers they have but need proper guidance to develop and reach their full potential. For many, the wilderness expedition is a way of learning to believe in oneself and move forward.

The following week I emailed Vicki to say that I was adding "Loving Me" to the Mission page of our foundation's website for others to read. It was then that she asked me if I had any plans to write a second book as she had an idea for one. I responded that I was focused on promoting *Walking With Jason* and the foundation but asked what was her idea. Her reply was most humbling. She felt her life's story would be an inspiration and help to others in like situations and asked if I would write her story.

It has been an honor to help Vicki put her story to paper. While a beautiful writer in her own right, Vick never felt she could write her life's story. She was too close and the experience would be too emotional. It was easier to tell me, a stranger, her story so I could write it down. We would meet and have to stop when the emotions overwhelmed her. The episodic emails that she would send were never written in one sitting; she would walk away, take a break, recover and continue. At times she has compared the process of telling her story to visiting the dentist office for a root canal or "pouring alcohol on an open wound." Sometimes the only way to get it all out was to just let it flow; let the writing happen without concern for grammar, spelling, etc. Think of opening a closet and letting all the hidden bones, all the terrible and shameful family secrets fall out. For Vicki the bones just didn't fall anywhere, they fell at the foot of the cross of Jesus and in the process she found forgiveness, healing, love and hope.

If Vicki had had one traumatic episode we would have probably written the book using the chapter format. A narrative would have been written of her life up to, during and following that trauma. Chapters would have been formed explaining her upbringing, so the reader could know who she was, as well as what happened in that specific event. But that is not how Vicki's life evolved. It wasn't one event. Rather, starting on the day she was born it has been one traumatic event after another. While at the same time Vicki met and experienced, as she calls them, God People and God Events.

It is a story best told without chapters which by their very nature force breaks. Breaks from the abuse were not something Vicki had. *Loving Me* is Vicki telling her story in a chronological flow of abuse. In reading her words it is hoped that the reader sees that one is not alone, help is there and exists in many different forms. Resources like social agencies, spiritual ministries and caring workshops are there ready to help. Dysfunctional families don't provide the safety blanket to wrap people in the love they need as God loves them. Help must come from outside the family, agencies which exist to support such victims as they move out of abuse and transform their lives.

Many who caused the pain, who traumatized Vicki, are dead. They can't be interviewed to ask why they did what they did; why they acted towards another human being with such viciousness. In this book we will not attempt to guess the reasons behind those actions, we will not attempt to retrace their lives as a way for Vicki to find healing. Of the living, her siblings and relatives, the impact of her family's dysfunctionality played out differently for each member to the point that some neither realize nor accept that they are victims as well. Having lived in the same house under the same parents her siblings have been impacted as well. They heard the arguments, heard the crying, and saw the abuse. They witnessed their dad drink away the food money as well as other dysfunctional events. They found ways to survive by locking those experiences away and trying to forget them but in the process they became traumatized themselves. Their lives today reflect the impact of that trauma and the futility of their attempts to lock it away.

Many have opposed Vicki's public discussions of her family life in the most unloving of ways. In their belief of "what happens in the family stays in the family." The generational curse is allowed to continue in their lives and in their relationships. This book is not about blaming others, it is not about accusing others and it is not about calling others out. Vicki's life has been impacted by what happened to her from the earliest of days of her life. This book focuses on how Vicki the victim has become the woman, the mother, the artist, the friend and the person she was always meant to be and continues to become today. This book shouts a line that we have heard time and again in our research, in our talks with the professionals who have helped Vicki along the way. It is this simple but powerful truth—**Each person has the innate creativity, has the means to change, to be what they were meant to be already inside themselves**! They may need coaching, they may need guidance, it may take time and effort as the challenges may be tough along the way but the ownership of the change and the strength to make the change are, from birth, within each of us.

One of the ways Vicki has learned to grow is by controlling her emotions rather than allowing the emotions to control her. A good example is when I emailed her my first attempt at writing this Foreword. She was first enveloped in various emotions competing for control, but she was able to step back, breathe deep, shed a tear or two, say a prayer and gain control of the emotions. Allowing her emotions to run amok was not an option; controlling her emotions allowed her "to offer hope and shine a light on a broken world."

In *Loving Me* Vicki doesn't get to finally face those who victimized her; she doesn't get her day in court. Vicki doesn't need any of that to heal. In fact, these perpetrators are irrelevant to her healing. We have read of others wanting such face to face moments in order to move on, for closure. But closure doesn't happen that way. It is not based on external events like a successful court trial that sends the rapist to prison or the actions of others like an abusing parent asking for forgiveness. Closure comes from within: completing the grieving process, accepting that the perpetrator/courts/other entities will not "get it" the way the victim wants. Closure for Vicki comes not in accepting the identity based on her traumatic life but on restoring her authentic identity, the identity she was born to be, and moving on in life and relationships.

The key to her healing, to her restoration, is dealing on a daily basis with the impact that these prior abuses have on her life now. While many of the perpetrators are dead it is the impact that lingers on, it is the impact that beats her down, and victimizes her. She truly is a victim or rather The Victim. The abuse put on her was not her fault; she did not ask to be abused, she did not ask to be born to a family that at birth called her "the ugliest kid." Vicki, in attempting to make sense of her abuse as the victim, especially happening as it did so early and so ongoing in her life lacked the emotional, spiritual, and mental capabilities to process the abuse. She thus took responsibility for the abuse and claimed it was her fault. Reasoning: "If it is my fault then I can make changes but if it is someone else's fault then I have no control of them and thus I will never heal." This thinking process turned into her identity of shame, of guilt and of being a bad person. The trauma became what she thought of herself. Vicki's challenge has been to overcome what Dr. Gary Sweeten E.D., Founder of LifeWay, calls "stinking thinking." In recognizing her victim status she frees herself from the illusion of fault and guilt.

This awareness of being the victim allows her to realize that she can restore her life to the fullest and not suspend herself as a survivor. Through her faith in God, through the care and support of some really good professionals, through working together in groups with other- like- victims, and through the love and support of her true friends, she has been able reach deep inside herself and draw on the innate strengths, values, and creative instincts she and all of us are born with to turn her life away from the life her parents lived and make a life that is Christ centered. She has escaped the generational curse of treating her children as her parents treated her, of exposing her children to the same hurtful life she experienced growing up.

Each of the following entries is based on Vicki's journals, interviews, and emails and speaks to the past. Once they were assembled I asked Vicki to review and comment based on what she knows now. Those comments are the Reflections found at the end of each entry.

John F. Hunt

Danielle Watkins

Preface

GROWING

We have all heard the saying that life is a journey. I definitely agree with that. Sometimes it is smooth sailing. Other times it is a fierce storm that invades when you least expect it and tears at your soul until you are sure there is nothing else left of you. But then the storm quiets and you are left lying on the shore of life, broken and beaten and wondering how you will ever recover.

Recovery is a choice. You might not want to ride the waves again, you might be thinking that no amount of sunshine will ever be worth the fierceness of the storms, but the only other choice you have is to continue to lay there lost and broken, and that is simply too uncomfortable.

So you make the decision to seek repair, to seek healing, to restore yourself to your original fullness. You look around at all the broken pieces and the mess that the storm has made and you have no idea where to start. Then you see something, someone out of the corner of your eye. It is Jesus, he is there picking up your broken pieces, brushing off the debris and looking at you with such love and concern. So together you rebuild.

After a trauma a "trauma identity" is formed. It is an identity of worthlessness, shame, guilt and other negatives. The process of my restoration is ongoing. It is a shifting from the unhealthy negative identity to the one of love, hope and happiness that God formed in creating me. I have to regain my ability to control my moods versus the moods controlling me.

As a man thinks in his heart, so is he. Proverbs 23:7

While the Bible is filled with joyful references to the importance of being grateful and thankful to God for whatever comes my way, even my traumas, science is now finding that my brain is complicit in my restoration. When I am being thankful the brain actually releases endorphins. When I am exercising gratitude the brain releases serotonins. These naturally occurring releases are in quantities equal to the respective dosages found in two very well-known pharmaceutical products. But submitting to God, trusting in him is hard work; changing what have become my core beliefs and my stinking thinking are a constant never ending task.

I have had to completely rebuild, relearn, regrow, and rethink. The destructive things that I learned as a child had to be removed and replaced with healing and love. In many ways I had to learn to grow up all over again.

Melissa Hannon

There is not a doubt in my mind that God sent my husband Jim in my life. The journeys he has taken with me, the storms he has rode out with me, the feelings, emotions that at times were all consuming, he embraced and weathered with me.

There are moments too when I resented Jim's ease at being ethical, responsible, honest, hardworking, loving, strong because I knew those were traits he was taught to have from his birth into adulthood. To him it was normal, to me it was foreign. His family dynamics were so different than mine were growing up.

So I came with some baggage…oh great is the love that when you come with some baggage he helps you unpack. And unpack we did. Every tear, every counseling session, every step of the way Jim has been there either physically or in spirit and always with love.

Even in our arguments, our moments of great pain, he stood firm in his love for me. And he has always been a reflection of God's love and how He wants us to love others. As I write this, I realize that I still have a lot of healing to do. I want to grow, heal, become, and flourish, and Jim encourages me to continue to grow. I always tease that when I grow up I want to be like Jim!

I have hurt Jim many times with my words because to be quite honest, I even needed to learn how to argue. Many times when I get angry or hurt I respond by going for the kill. I spit out hateful, hurtful words faster than a machine gun spits out rounds. I learned that trait and it is awful and unnecessary. I am getting better at speaking my feelings, instead of striking out in fear. I have the fear of confrontation. I hate it! But I am continually learning that I can speak my mind or better my feelings without being abusive. There is such a thing as righteous anger that is being angry at something or someone without abuse.

When you look at the example Jesus gives, when He went in and turned the merchant tables over that were in the temple. He turned the tables over; in his anger and disgust he said this cannot be! I don't remember him calling any of those men names. I don't remember him striking them with abuse or insults. He was angry and he did turn the tables over and yell "Get out!" But all the names he could have called them, all the truths about these men He could have spoken, but He didn't. He was angry without abuse physically or verbally. I want to give Jim respect. I will forever work on getting better and better at that. Love should be respectful.

In my meetings with my counselor Sandy Morgenthal, Med, LPCC-S, CCFC, RN, she has helped me realize that to find true joy, peace and contentment I need to:
1. Surrender my will to God.
2. Be sure, if not quick, to forgive.
3. Intentionally come to a spiritual kind of acceptance, not drudgingly but willfully.
4. Have good boundaries.

Telling my story is not an easy thing to do. I heard it said that everyone has skeletons in their closets. I don't know if that is true or not. I do know that it is extremely hard to open up the closet door and let all the skeletons fall out in front of everyone! But pretending they are not there doesn't work for long. You are always aware of their presence and the only true way to move on is to let the skeletons fall at the feet of Jesus. Only His love is big enough, forgiving enough, and pure enough to truly make all things new. There is no judgment at the feet of Jesus, only love. At the feet of Jesus I find my comfort. I find true love there and I find healing there. There are those who will argue that fact and ask where Jesus was when I was being abused or broken. Where was Jesus when my dad was trying to kill my mom? Where was Jesus in the violence and the pain? So many questions.....Where? Why? The questions beat on us like the winds of a terribly violent storm. I answer that with this: "Jesus was on the cross." The day that Jesus was on the cross all my pain, suffering, shame, sin, heartache, hatred, anger was on his body. Every tear I have ever cried, every sin I have ever committed and every sin that was committed against me was on him. All of it, the severe ugliness of it all was on Him. He carried it, He felt it, He cried out in the anguish of it all and He bled and died in the weight of it all. He loved me enough to carry my sins and the sins of those who hurt me. He loved us all enough to carry the sins of the world. So every tear I have ever cried, every painful moment I have ever experienced He has already experienced. He has been in that moment before me and His love carries me through every experience I have had or will ever have. I may cry and feel the pain but, there will also always be a comfort there. There is an unshakable, unending power of His love and presence in every moment of every day. When I look back now I can see just how His love carried me. God's great love for me always amazes me.

He bore my griefs and carried my sorrows and by his stripes I am healed. Isaiah 53: 4-5

I know there are memories that I have blocked out. Missing pieces. I think it is a protective device from God. Only He knows what we can handle and at what pace. It has taken me 53 years to get this far. I think recovery will be something I will always be working on. I want to grow and be all that God has intended for me to be. Mostly I want to have self-worth and really, deeply believe that I am lovable and that God loves me. I know this in my brain, but the shame factor, the "stinking thinking" is still there and I am learning how to really believe this in my heart.

In reading the first draft of this book, I experience some unexpected emotions. One was fear! It started to rise up in my chest and my first reaction was to call John and scream "No! We can't do this! This is just too ugly, too painful, too much!"

Then after some deep breathing I tried to identify where these emotions were coming from and immediately the word "family" came to mind. I have always sought their acceptance. I have always longed for their unconditional love and I realized that if any sibling or family member were to read this book, they were going to get mad! Plenty mad!

How dare I talk about my parents, my life, and my abuse! How dare I open the closet door and let the skeletons fall! The old tapes started playing and I could hear their voices and see the fingers pointing and they were screaming at me....Liar! Whore! Over-reactor! And I cowered down in my seat and longed to run and turn my back and say it is better left in the dark. But then, the light was too bright and the light and the darkest couldn't co-exist and I couldn't, I wouldn't give up the light. So I sat and waited and breathed deep breaths and I cried a few tears. I prayed: "Let this light illuminate the whole earth and try to put it out. I will roar like a lion!" This book is not meant to slander people, but to offer hope and to shine the light on a broken world, to show others in pain that they can grow, that they can find help and they can find healing.

Vicki Watkins

Acknowledgments

My life story is what it is. The facts as I know them shaped my life in ways that another should not have to experience. Unfortunately, others will. I pray they find support and strength to face their inner demons as I have. In acknowledging that support I ask those in need of help to look for help in your specific town or home city. Support is available everywhere in one shape or another. Don't stop looking.

To those who stepped into my life and showed me another way I am forever grateful: Paula Wilkerson my lifetime friend; Ann Sikes my surrogate mother; Dr. Pamela Hanson who saved me during my most dangerous and vulnerable moment. Thank you for being there when I needed you the most.

Many of the words I use in describing my inner wounds are words I learned in therapy. Words I have absorbed to give me the deeper understanding into the help needed to restore myself. In writing this book I have relied heavily on the words of my friends, teachers and life supporters: Dr. Gary Sweeten, E.D. of Sweeten Life Systems and founder of the LifeWay Holistic Adult Counseling Program of Emerson North Hospital who saved me from suicide and began the process of restoring me to whom I was created to be; Rebecca Born, MSW, LISW, and Rachel Davis, MS, CFLE, co-founders of Connections, A Safe Place and their social work groups for helping me make the deep belief

systems exchanges; Sandy Morgenthal, Med, LPCC-S, CCFC, RN of
Professional Pastoral-Counseling Institute for her continuing support
and counseling.

I could not write this, I could not begin to expose myself without my
husband Jim, always at my side, always supporting me, always loving me.

PART ONE

Laura Kagawa Burke

No snares are ever so insidious as those lurking as dutiful devotion or labeled as family affection. You can easily escape from an open foe, but when hatred lurks in the bosom of a family it has taken a position and pounced upon you before it can be spied out or recognized for what it is.
Cicero

And a man's enemies will be those of his own household.
Matthew 10:36

My Life Today

I am in Maine, sitting on a sailboat with Jim and Danielle. Watching the waves cra sh gently against the boat, I can feel the sun on my face and there is a gentle breeze blowing. Across the waves I spot a seal, his head peeking out of the water. Up and down his head bobs like he is playing a game of peek-a-boo. He is adorable! And he makes me smile. He makes me want to play too.

It is so peaceful here. The waves are gently rocking me and I can feel the presence of God. His creation and beauty surrounds me and at this moment all is well.

The last few years have been a struggle. My illness has tried so hard to defeat me. The pain and fear still come when I have an attack, but now this moment the reminders of my illness, of my past are swept away in the caress and beauty of the ocean.

My husband Jim and my daughter Danielle and I are on vacation in Maine. This vacation has been a long time coming. Twenty three years of waiting. From the time we first married Jim and I always talked about going to Maine. From the time I was a little girl I dreamed about Maine. I have read about it over the years, heard about it and it became a dream of mine. I have had a lot of dreams over the years, some small ones, some big. At times they all seemed impossible to reach. But for the most part, my dreams have come true.

Today I am sailing on the Atlantic Ocean in Maine. I can walk. I can get around better than I ever did just a few years ago. My brain tumor is gone. I am safe from abuse. I am loved and accepted by my kids, husband and friends. I have a wonderful personal relationship with Jesus. I have a good support system, a wonderful counselor (Sandy). I own an Art Gallery/Store "Under the Stars" in Batavia, Ohio. I have had my book of poetry published and I am currently working on my autobiography with my friend and author John Hunt.

My yesterdays are gone. The pain has left its scars, but through the love of God, I have woven those scars into a beautiful tapestry of my life. The pain adds color, shapes and dimensions that only when mixed with love can become all things good.

I have never had a halo, but if I did it would be tarnished and have many dents in it; tarnished by all the prideful rain that I allowed to fall on it. Dents from the many times God had to knock it off my head to remind me that He paid the price for my freedom and it wasn't anything I ever did on my own.

No, I have never had a halo although people often look for me to have one. For when I say Jesus is the son of God and my Savior then people look for my halo. They expect me to be perfect. When I don't live up to their interpretation on what a believer should be, then they are disappointed that I don't have a halo that they can knock off.

I have never had a halo, but I do have grace. And the grace that has been given me shines brightly for the world to see and no matter how hard anyone tries to knock the grace out of me, they can't! There will never be any dents in my grace because God's grace is perfect and permanent.

Grace is much more beautiful than a halo because grace is nothing that I accomplished, but everything that I am.

Today I sail the ocean blue, yesterday I cried for you. This is my story. This is how I got here.

PART TWO

The Golden Thread of Hope

The golden thread of hope hangs from Heaven to me

And reminds me of my future when I'm too blind to see

The golden thread of hope helps me hold my head up high

Even in the worse of storms I have its peace inside

For nothing can break or sever this thread

Nothing among the living or among the dead

The golden thread of hope is woven with His love

And keeps my focus not on this world, but on things above

The golden thread of hope, though invisible to some

Keeps my eyes on where I'm going, not on where I'm from

The golden thread of hope that I hold in my hand

Reminds me that I am loved and part of God's great plan

Vicki Watkins 2015

Good v. Evil

John Martino

1961 – The Ugliest Kid You Ever Had

Reprint of Vicki's Baby Book

I WAS BORN on March 17, 1961. I often wonder what my mother was feeling as she held me, her newborn daughter in her arms. Certainly there must have been some joy while looking down at the new daughter she had given birth to and it is probably safe to say that she also felt fear. Fear because now she had yet another child by her husband, the man who she both hated and loved; the man who brought terror into her life almost on a daily basis. Here in her arms she held yet another anchor to a man and a life that she so much wanted to escape from.

Lily was forced to work or claim welfare as Ed, my dad, was never around. She tried selling cleaning supplies door-to-door while my older brother and sister were little. She was dependent on others as she never learned to drive. Lily was very naïve and without a high school education living in a city that was so different from her rural Kentucky roots. She grew up believing men owned women. She never told anyone what was happening to her – the abuse, the fear; her husband really messed her up.

My Mom had very, very strict parents. Growing up she had rules placed on her and so she did the opposite raising my siblings and me – no rules. Also my dad controlled her which meant she never had any balance in her life. She always claimed she trusted us to do right, trusted us to be good kids. But she never explained what right was or what a good kid did. She never talked about things like growing up, doing right, or even having a period. There was no parental example of how to live. Sometimes I think growing up in the mountain valleys of Kentucky did not prepare my parents or any of their siblings for life in the city. My parents and most of their siblings were all dysfunctional. Uncle B, Ed's brother and drinking binge partner once threw an axe at his son's back; another time he tried to burn the house down with the family inside. My mom's sister "Birdie" was a mean alcoholic. It seemed the only thing Lily learned growing up was that men were in charge. Ed reinforced this lesson.

Maybe for a minute she was foolish enough to think that this baby could make him change. But if she thought that, it was only for a moment because sadly she knew by now that he would never change. Did she feel anger? Was she angry at the thought of another mouth to feed and more responsibility and she knew in her heart that my father would never take care of me. Did she smile or did she cry? By this time, she already had two older children by him and 15 years of an abusive marriage. By then was she even of capable of knowing her own feelings?

In my baby book under the remarks page my mother wrote her first thought of me "How ugly." She also wrote what my dad said the first time he saw me. He said, "Ugliest kid you ever had." Maybe those two lines say it all. Maybe from that day forward I began to feel ugly, unloved and lost. And I certainly didn't know then that it would take me over 50 years to really believe that I was a beautiful being created by God.

By the time I was born my mother had been beaten and abused by my father several times. They had been separated several times, only to reunite with a false hope of change given to her. Each time she went back, she went back with a heart full of hope and fear. Each time she went back, she felt like there was no other choice. The beatings, the pain, the sexual abuse, the adultery, the death threats, the horror continued and she endured and lost a little bit of herself with each blow.

Her God given potential was stripped away by a vicious man and the fact that she never sought help in healing both emotionally and spiritually. She was no longer the person God had intended for her to be but had become what a violent man and unhealed wounds had made her.

It certainly didn't help the situation that I was a very sick baby. By 1965 I had under gone three major surgeries. In June of 1962 I had brain tumor surgery. I had a benign brain tumor removed from behind my right ear. I was in the hospital thirty days. When I got out there was a thin skin covering over the incision sight and it could get punctured. So my mom had to be very careful and watch me. In January of 1964 I went back into Children's Hospital to have another skull operation. This time the doctor took a bone from my skull and put it over the opening in my head. Then in June of 1965 I had a tumor growing on the end of my spine and I had to have that removed.

My mother and I always had a love hate relationship. She could be funny and silly and make me laugh and she could turn in a moment and be angry and screaming and throwing things. It was confusing to me as a child and I found myself trying to please her. I loved her dearly and I loved the side of her that made me a nurse cap out of a paper napkin, the side that sang silly songs and told silly stories. I even loved the side of her that threw things at me and verbally insulted me and expected so much from such a young child.

My mother never learned to drive and she didn't go anywhere by herself. By the time I was ten years old, my father was living in a different state and only came back periodically to haunt us

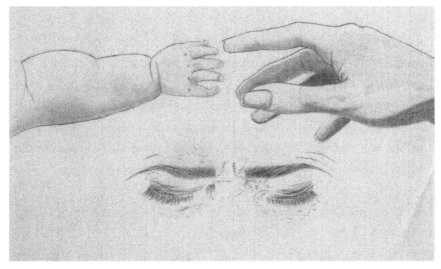

Olivia Killebrew

with physical threats and abuse. I remember my father would come to Ohio, get drunk in a bar and then he would call my mother on the phone to threaten her. He would scream in his drunken slur that he was coming over to kill her and all of us. My mom would call my older brother for a ride or a neighbor and together my mother and my younger brother and I would ride over to my older sister's apartment to hide out. My sister was married at the time and we would stay there until somehow mom had learned the threat had passed and dad was arrested or gone and it was safe to return.

REFLECTION

When I look back at this now it makes me sad: Sad that my sister and I weren't loved and favored like the boys. Sad that running from a death threat from my father was a normal part of my childhood. It is sad because I now know how critical a mother's support is as an indicator of how a child will recover from sexual abuse and how that child will grow in a healthy way. In fact from what I have learned the depth of a mother's love is the most effective predictor of a child's ability to recover than any other factor. It is sad because my mom could not get the help she needed to recover from her abuse to be able to help us, her daughters, recover from ours. It is sad because there wasn't a supportive parent to turn to, to ask for help.

What is most sad is that the stage was already set on the day of my birth. Without supportive and positive parents, without the ability to tell someone, being abused by both and fearing to tell either one about the other, my future, the potential for my wellbeing, my mental and emotional health were dramatically altered. Modern clinical surveys now attest to what my life bears witness to the lack of a supportive non-abusive parent destroyed my self-worth and weakened my ability to develop healthy interpersonal adjustments and relationships.

Laura Kagawa-Burke

Palaces

From the moment I first met you, you hated me.

I don't know what it was that I did exactly.

Maybe I said something wrong

Or did something stupid

Or maybe it was just a random spin of the wheel that brought me
here.

Whatever the reason, here I am

It was decided, you would play the king, and I the hapless fool.

You had your knights to defend you, your court all around you

And I, I was there to make you laugh

And laugh you did.

I heard from my friends the cook and the scullery maid how you'd
been insulting me

At first I was confused.

I started to wonder what I had done.

So I tried to act calmer

I tried to play it cool

I tried to act like I was a queen stuck in the body of a fool

But it didn't work

Your palace was made of fool's gold and every wall had a fun house
mirror hanging on it

And every time I walked through your world I couldn't keep my eyes
from the walls

Comparing what I saw in the reflection to the pyrite all around me.

I've since grown smarter.

And so I have an announcement

I am leaving

Leaving behind your palace built by idiots and I am going to build
my own, as a wiser idiot

You see, your palace is built on a fault line

On a convergent boundary where two crashing plates of hate and
     pain come together
And I can feel the pressure building up and I'm no seismologist but
     I can tell that an earthquake's coming and I'm not gonna be here
     when it hits
I'm going to build my own palace.
My palace won't be built of bricks or stone
It will be as flimsy as a willow tree and that is okay
Because when the wind comes I'd rather be a willow tree that bends
     than an oak tree that breaks
'Cause the wind always comes, and the wind is always welcome
At least by me
Because the wind will blow away all else until there is nothing left but
     what was there before
Before you and before me
And before you hurt me
The wind always comes after to bring back what was before
And before I go further I would like to mention the roof of my palace
That is to say I would like to, but I can't because it doesn't exist
My palace has no roof
Which may seem like a flaw in the construction, but let me assure
     you, it was completely intentional
Because I love the rain
Rain is inevitable and you can either avoid it, or you can run in it
Letting the water wash over you and clean your wounds 'cause God
     knows you've got a lot of them
And nothing is better than playing in a puddle
And nothing can hide tears better than a rain cloud
And I've got a lot of tears to hide
Speaking of hiding, I would like to offer this peace treaty to the entire
     world
I am so tired of war

I have hidden all of my weapons in my royal armory and sealed it
    with a key which I promptly lost
And I don't plan on looking for it.
I'm done with fighting and I'm ready to start breathing again
And I am ready to start living again
And living should not be an uphill battle but an under-the-sea
    expedition in search of glorious things
But so many people get lost in this imaginary war that they forget
    how to swim and end up drowning
And there aren't enough boats in my fleet to save them all
So I will welcome anyone into my palace.
And if you come in and there is there is no chair for you to sit on I
    will gladly offer you my throne and will sit upon the floor
Sit upon the dragon- scale tiled floor which I made myself
Because I've fought my fair share of dragons and it's about time that I
    start cleaning up the mess.
And in my palace the doors are always open and anyone may walk
    through them, myself included
And above every doorway in my palace will hang a plaque that
    therein says every lie you ever told me and every lie I ever told
    myself
So that I am always reminded of where I have been, but that I am
    always moving past it.
Because the past is too far behind me and the future too far away for
    me to worry about either of them anymore
I am not a queen
And I am not a fool
But I am a knight, and I don't want to fight a war but I would die to
    defend this palace.
Because this is a sacred place.
Not the kind of place where you have to take your shoes off to enter
Or splash water on your face to see.
But a place of unsuppressed reality and unreasonable dreaming

PART TWO   17

Which surprisingly, work really well together
And it is this paradox that keeps my flimsy palace standing.
Because I know that the world is cruel
And I know that wars will be fought
Plagues will come
Lies will be told
And my palace might fall
But I know that it might not
And that, that's what keeps my palace upright
Because I am willing and ready to fall
Because at least when I fall I will know that I was standing.

DANIELLE WATKINS 2015

REFLECTION

My daughter Danielle is an amazing writer. She wrote this after an experience she had with bullying. It fit so well with my story too. This is so beautiful and like this poem says "I've fought my fair share of dragons and it's about time that I start cleaning up the mess."

1962 Brain Tumor #1

I HAD BRAIN tumor surgery in June, 1962. I had a benign brain tumor removed from behind my right ear. I was in Children's hospital for 30 days. My dad never came to visit. In fact my cousin Ray had to drive my mom to hospital because dad was off on a drunken binge somewhere. When I got out there was a thin skin covering over the incision site and I had to be watched very carefully because it could be punctured.

1963 Oscar

THE CONSTANT CRYING from an unhealthy baby, the abuse from a violent husband and the fear of each day had taken its toll on my mother. So when she met Oscar, a bar owner, a man that gave her the attention she longed for and helped her financially with groceries and other needs, the affair must have felt like a rescue to her, but of course it wasn't. I have only heard the stories of my mother's affair with this man, some from my mom herself and some from my older sister who is thirteen years older than me. I have two pictures of this man that my mom pasted in my baby book. I am sitting with mom and Oscar and I look to be about 3 years old. Although he did help mom with groceries, financial needs and pretty dresses and toys for me, he did not come without his own baggage. He was an alcoholic and a drug user and although he never hit my mother, he did have alcoholic binges and he certainly was not an emotionally healthy person to be around or to have a small child around. He bit me once while he was drunk. I was about two years old and Oscar was lying in his bed very drunk. Mom was getting ready to leave from her visit with him and was holding me on her hip. She bent over so he could kiss me goodbye and he bite into my left breast hard! My older sister was there and witnessed it. To this day I still have the scar on my breast. Sometimes I look back and wonder why my mother continued to see this man and continued to have me around him. I know that she felt like she needed him and she wanted him in her life. She put that need before her child's. I can safely assume that most of the male figures around me were not safe men to be around.

REFLECTION

When I think of Oscar and my dad today I get an uneasy feeling. It is not that I hate these men. The memories of them make me uncomfortable. Many years later my dad would quit drinking and go to church. But I never wanted to be alone with him and as an adult I never was. I didn't see him often because he lived in another state. I had forgiven him but I didn't trust him.

To forgive does not mean I forget the abuse nor does it mean I can reconcile with those that abused me. Rather forgiveness gives me the freedom to move on. I was the one stuck while my perpetrators lived their lives. They could care less but I, I had the shame, I had the guilt, I had stinking thinking.

Trust was hard for me to understand. I trusted the wrong people to love me, to help me. I had to learn to rely on my gut instincts and learn to trust them. I needed to develop my 6th sense for people but I was getting too many wrong messages to process.

1964 Follow-up Operation

IN JANUARY, I went back to Children's hospital to have an operation to build up and cover where the tumor had been removed. The doctor took a bone from my skull and put it over the soft spot opening in my head.

1964 Ed

ONE OF MY earliest memories of dad is when I am 3 or 4 years old. I am hungry and my mom is making me a scrambled egg. I am sitting in a chair waiting for it. My father comes in the kitchen. He is drunk, he has a gun. He forces my mother into the bedroom at gun point. He shuts the bedroom door and locks it. I am standing outside the bedroom door crying because I want my egg. I know something is wrong because I can't open the bedroom door and my mother won't come to me. Our phone is ringing. My oldest sister is running up the stairs to our second floor apartment.

I found out later as an adult that my dad had been out with my Uncle B (also an abusive alcoholic) that day drinking. Uncle B and a couple of his sons were parked across the street watching the house while my father went inside to try and kill my mother.

Sissy, my oldest sister (13-years older) was walking up the street toward our home coming from the neighborhood store. She was walking with a friend when she spotted my uncle sitting in his car across the street. She knew there was trouble. She dropped her bag and took off running toward our home, yelling at her friend to call the police. She found me outside the bedroom door crying and mom locked in the bedroom with my dad and his gun.

Meanwhile my Aunt Jennie had been trying to call my mom. That was why the phone was ringing. My aunt had found out that Uncle B and my dad were back in town and was calling to warn my mom. When no one answered the phone she called the police too.

My sister saved my mom's life that day. She kept banging on the door yelling at dad that the police were on their way and he would get arrested. I am not sure of what entirely my father did to my mom that day. I would hear stories later in life. It is one of the many stories that Ed beat her and probably assaulted her. The cops came and arrested him. But in those days, domestic violence wasn't looked upon like it is today. My dad would get taken in often, but always released later to come back and hurt again. Sometimes dad would stay gone on drunken binges for days or weeks, other times not.

But my sister and I were not protected, especially my sister. My Uncle B was an alcoholic and a horrible abusive man (he once threw an axe through his son's back). My Uncle C was an alcoholic. My sister has told me stories of being in bed with my Uncle C and he had her play with him.

REFLECTION

When I think about this event now I realize how at such an early age I was introduced to fear and violence. The stranglehold of fear would have its talons hooked into me my entire life. Example: On a slow day at the store I own I will start to panic. The spirit of fear will manifest and I will repeat the following verse.

> *For God has not given us the spirit of fear, but of power, and of love, and of a sound mind.* 2 Timothy 1:7

Fear is good if it warns you of an immediate threat and lets you adjust to protect yourself. But I began to live a life of constantly thinking that

I was in danger, thinking that I needed to be alert at all times and that I was powerless to stop it. This false sense of protection was unhealthy because I could not distinguish when I was really in danger; I had no way of gauging a threat. My whole life was on high alert.

1964 Babysitter

ONE OF ELEVEN siblings, he was twenty-two and Lily was twenty-one when they married in 1946 They moved to Cincinnati, Ohio, from the Somerset area of Kentucky in 1947. I grew up thinking his life was normal: his drinking binges with his brother Uncle B, his affairs, and his inability to hold a job for long. He never supported the family, never sent birthday cards, never gave gifts and never was home to celebrate with the family.

He was extremely violent. He would call home from a bar, drunk, and threaten to come home and kill us all. He once came home so drunk that he hung the babysitter out the second story window by her ankles until she told him where my mom hid the food money. Another time he took my brother Kent to the grocery store with the food money. But he stopped at a bar and drank it all. On the way home he found a pigeon, killed it and cooked it. He warned Kent not to say anything; my brother could not eat that night.

Finally in 1964 after holding a gun to my mom he was sent to Rollmans Psychiatric Institute. My sister, Sissy, saved my mom several times. Sissy told her high school counselor the whole story who reported dad to Social Services. Sissy was removed and lived with Aunt "Pug" for a while. While at Rollmans he wrote Lily a letter asking if Uncle B and the boys "got hauled away." But he could not remember why he was there. Once out he would visit on occasion more like a stranger. Each time Ed came back Lily and he would fight incessantly. His visits seemed to be kept to a minimum but with each visit was the fear of what he would do next.

Lily would use my sister Sissy as a decoy. When Ed came home drunken Sissy would ask for a piggyback ride so she could search his pockets for money so mom could buy groceries. Other times Lily would send Sissy into the bar where dad was drinking to ask him for money. For a while mom would claim she was taking Sissy to see friends when she was really connecting with Oscar but it didn't last. When Ed went to Rollmans, Oscar left as well. Maybe he was afraid that Lily would want him to support her and the family completely. In the end Sissy was blamed for opening the family secrets to Social Services. Sissy could not catch a break. I have a photograph of Ed, Sissy & myself; at least I think it is Sissy. Looking at the picture no one will know for sure because she scratched her face out of the picture. She could not bear to be part of the moment.

Today Sissy has a hard time admitting what happened, but the scars exist. Sissy cannot drive by herself, cannot pump gas nor buy milk! Married at 19 she never had a social life, Fred was her knight in shining armor but she never had any help learning what to do. Then her marriage fell apart when Fred got his teenage girlfriend pregnant and left to marry her. Counselors will tell you that a child traumatized remains emotionally at the child's age at the time of the trauma. That is Sissy; she hasn't been able to move forward, to grow, and to develop.

My dad was always a smart dresser. I don't ever remember seeing him in jeans or t-shirts or any casual clothes. He didn't hold a job very long. Sometimes he worked for his brother on his brother's farm. Even then he wore dress slacks and a button down shirt. That was as casual as he got. My mom would complain that they wouldn't have money for food, but dad always dressed nice!

That old saying, "Never judge a book by its cover" is true. My dad slept around with women, a lot. He would go to the bars and pick them up. He would bring them home and introduce these lady friends to my mom. He told these ladies that my mom was his sister and he would take the lady into his bedroom and they would spend the night. My mom was too afraid of my dad to say anything or to tell the lady that she was his wife. He did this often. That was how great my mom's fear was of my dad.

He even had a girlfriend named Lee. My mom called her "Hopping Lee" because she had a hop in her step.

Another time he actually got shot in the leg by the husband of a woman with whom he was having an affair!

REFLECTION

I believe my parents did accept the Lord as their savior, in that they certainly did believe Jesus died on the cross for them, but I strongly doubt that they sought recovery from all that hindered them. I don't even know if they knew they needed help and recovery. I can't speak for them. I know that both of them had a dark side and that side brought great pain and heartache to me.

I don't harbor bitterness or anger toward them. In my own healing I have learned how to let that go. Now there are times when a memory comes back and the anger and the pain swell up inside of me. At those moments I am angry and I hate them. But I have learned and am still learning to go to God in prayer. I write in my journal a lot. I exercise. I hit pillows. I walk. I read my Bible. I help others. Whatever it takes, don't want any of those dark feelings, that "stinking thinking" to ever take root in me.

Yes I have forgiven them and yes I still get angry and mad for what they have done to me and for failing to protect me. The emotions are real. To forgive was an intentional act on my part while my showing of anger is a natural automatic response of my emotions expressing themselves. He gives me the space to understand those emotions.

1964 Ed

THIS WAS TOLD to me by Sissy.

I am probably 3 or 4 years old because it happened on Adams Ave. in Norwood. That is where we lived when my brother Joe was born. Joe wasn't born yet and I am 4 years and 8 months older than Joe.

Dad was hung over from drinking the night before. Mom had a footstool but the material had come undone. She and Sissy were trying to fix it. Mom was hammering on the footstool while Sissy was trying to hold the material down.

Dad told mom to stop hammering. Mom hammered one more time and dad jumped up and started choking mom. Mom was on the floor and dad was choking her. Sissy a young teenager jumped on dad's back, trying to get him off of mom. Dad grabbed Sissy by the hair and threw her across the room onto the bed. Sissy doesn't remember what exactly happened next.

REFLECTION

As I write this I can't help but think of my 17 year old daughter Danielle. Her life is all about her friends, and school, school dances and activities and her cat, that she adores! Her greatest concern might be about an upcoming test, or if her face breaks out with a pimple. She is the typical, happy teenager.

How different her teen years are from Sissy's teen years or mine: The horror of watching your dad trying to harm or kill your mom; the neglect, verbal and physical abuse. Sissy and I both have our memories in some ways different, in many ways the same. No one was looking out for Sissy and no one was looking out for me.

1965 Spine Tumor

I HAD A tumor or growth growing on the end of my spine and I had that removed.

1965 Joe

MY YOUNGEST BROTHER was born in December of 1965. My mother adored him. Since he was a male, I think my mother saw him as someone that maybe someday could really help rescue her from the life she had lived and of course he was the baby. He was so cute, with chubby cheeks and he was her favorite from day one and we all knew it. He could do no wrong in my mother's eyes. He never suffered from mom's darker side. He never became a victim of it and he never understood that it did exist. But he lived in that environment, he saw things and because of that I sometimes fear he has an issue with alcohol. One of his kids has been in jail for drug abuse. The generational curse continues for his family.

REFLECTION

Every child has the natural instinct to survive. Each child unconsciously refuses to accept the painful reality and thus builds a wall around one's self to shut out the pain and to protect. But in denying the reality and intentionally staying in that denial only leads to more pain and unfulfilled potential.

1965 Ed

I AM LYING in bed about 4 years old. I saw my dad standing over the bed; he was looking at me and mom. Mom is lying next to me asleep. (I am in their bed with mom) Sissy (my sister) is on a roll away bed beside their bed. Daddy got in bed. He had been out drinking. He reeked of alcohol. He was drunk. I was glad to see him. Daddy held me and cuddled me, it felt nice. Then daddy started rubbing me, touching me. He wants me to touch him. I didn't want to, but I wanted to make daddy happy and this makes him happy. Mom slept on and so did Sissy in the roll away bed next to us. Afterwards daddy was asleep too.

REFLECTION

Today I own an art gallery. Our basement is a beautiful used bookstore. 50% of all proceeds from the bookstore each month go to the House of Peace Domestic Violence Center here in Clermont County. I wanted a way to give something to help women today. Unfortunately domestic violence is still very real even today. The consequences of domestic violence can go way beyond the abused spouse. The crippling effects of domestic violence can be felt many generations later if not addressed.

10 million children are exposed to domestic violence annually. DV is the #3 cause of homelessness. The #1 reason the victim stays in 98% of domestic violence cases is financial abuse - a lack of financial resources to break free. Domestic violence accounts for over 70% of all female

murders in this country. The jilted lover or the husband feels that he losing control which to a man is his validation. For a man to be rejected in love is a sign of losing power. Such a loss leads to frustration and eventually anger. If that anger builds it may lead to revenge and no restraining order, no judge's order or police promise of protection can stop a man from hurting the woman who attacked his manhood.

A woman is at her greatest danger of physical harm when she tells him she is leaving him. Domestic violence workers constantly advise women to leave if they must but to keep their whereabouts secret! Battered women shelters try to keep their locations secret for fear of reprisals. Society needs to allow men to learn to process their feelings in a constructive manner; they need to learn to cope with feeling inadequate and helpless without blaming others for what went wrong. Women will talk to their friends but men keep it all buttoned up inside.

References:

Queen City Notorious JT Townsend 2014 Virtuaklbookworm.com College Station, TX pg 222

30 Shocking Domestic Violence Statistics That Remind us it's An Epidemic Huffingtonpost.com October 23, 2014

1968 Ed

DIFFERENT CULTURES, SOCIETIES have different ways of life. There's an old saying: different strokes for different folks.

My parents grew up in the hills of Kentucky. I grew up in the city. I have no idea how my parents were brought up. I know that both grew up in strict homes. My mom especially grew up in poverty; most likely my dad did too.

My father always had beagle dogs, as long as I can remember. He had them at my grandparents' place. He had them at his place when he lived in Kentucky. He had them when he lived in Lockland, Ohio. He would buy them, trade them, and sell them. He was really into the whole beagle dog trade.

I am a little girl about 7 years old. I am on my grandparents' farm in Kentucky visiting my dad. He is living with them at the time. A beagle had puppies. I am not certain, but I think one is a runt. I don't know, but for whatever reason they "aren't any good." Dad has what looks like a hammer. Looking back at it now, it was probably a club of some kind.

I remember the puppies aren't moving anymore and there is blood. I am standing by dad as he puts them in a plastic bag. I remember being scared. Later dad throws the bag with the dead puppies in it out into a big pond. I am standing there as he throws the bag. "They weren't no good," he says. I think about those puppies for a long, long time after that. I wish the puppies would have been good!

1968 Joy

LILY WAS NEVER a protector of the girls as she was with her sons. When Kent, my oldest brother by 14 years, was draft age Lily swore he was her sole support which kept him out of the draft. It wasn't until Kent married Joy that I felt someone cared about me. She was younger than my brother so she wasn't as distant. She would buy me clothes, fix my hair and pay me attention that I never had before. She had a loving heart and would stop Lily's rages and beatings. She loved to read; it is because of her that I do as well. I would read the text books cover to cover; it was and still is to this day a great escape. My reading inspired my journaling which I have continued to this day. But I needed glasses and have always felt I was ugly in my glasses.

1969 Ed

I AM ABOUT eight years old. Dad is living in an apartment in Lockland, Ohio. He has a roommate. I am over there to visit. The roommate has been drinking I can smell it on him. Dad smells like alcohol too.

I am spending the night. Dad wants me to hold his private part. I remember him putting my hand on it. That is all I remember.

The next day dad says, "Don't tell your mom we were drinking. Don't tell your mom about our secret."

I am scared. I am sad.

REFLECTION
To this day I hate the smell of alcohol. I hate being around it. I always feel unsafe being around it. It is one more thing I have to work on healing from.

The brain is an amazing gift from God, even at age 7 when not fully developed. The emotions working with the brain store information about events. This information filters future events as a means of protection. Neuron pathways carry messages about what is a good and what is a bad experience. A sound, a sight, a taste, a feel and a smell can trigger the brain into defense mode. My senses are constantly feeding my sensory thalamus with sensory information. That data is sent via separate pathways to the amygdala, which tags the event to one of my emotions, and to the hippocampus which stores the data and forwards it. The cortex receives this data, analyzes it, and makes decisions. Every new experience creates it owns wiring system based upon all previous experiences. All of this runs smoothly and automatically until the amygdala tags an event as a threat or danger. The amygdala immediately short circuits the system, overrides the cortex, takes control of the body and sends it into high alert.

The word emotion is derived from the Latin word meaning "to move out" and the body's response is just that: to fight, to take flight, to freeze or to faint. The energy the body brings to this event is incredible and needs to be released. Looking back I realize now that my living under constant threat forced me to insulate myself from the alerts and the events by holding that energy inside. Because this energy had no way to vent it found other more destructive ways to play out throughout my life. The journey or restoration is tough. It is a process. The dictionary defines process as a series of actions directed towards a specific aim. I aim at having Rational Christian Thinking. To believe the truth of God and not the lies told to me. I aim to grow and heal. I aim to constantly believe that I am never alone!

1969 Lily

I AM VERY young, about eight years old. My little brother and I shared a room. We had two twin beds in the room; each of us sleeps in our own bed. I have a terrible nightmare, someone… something is hurting me. I wake up crying. I am very, very scared. I climb out of bed and run into my mom's room which is right next to mine. I stand by her bed crying. I had a bad dream, I sob. I try to climb into bed with mom. She won't let me. She pushes me back and yells, "Get back in your own bed now!" I am crying really hard, but mom is getting aggravated and swats me on the tail. "Get back in your bed!" she demands.

I go back. I try to turn the light on, but she is yelling, "Turn off that light." I don't know how she knows I am trying to turn a light on.

I go over to my little brother's bed. He is sleeping soundly. I climb up in bed with him, so scared and not wanting to be alone. "Get out of your brother's bed right now," mom screams.
She knows I tried to get in to his bed.

I go back to my bed, in the dark. I am sitting on my bed sobbing. It is so dark in the room. Mom comes into the room. "I told you to quit crying, you big baby! I'll give you something to cry about," she yells. Then she goes back to her bed.

Sometimes I still have nightmares, especially if I am stressed. Sometimes I scream so loud I wake up my husband or my daughter. They always wake me up if they hear me in the middle of one. Sometimes they will give me a hug. Sometimes I turn the light on. Sometimes I just need a few minutes to relax and breathe.

I am not alone. God always comforts. When I say my evening prayers I ask God not to allow the nightmares, but if they have to come, I ask that God be right there with me in the nightmare. I learned that from my counselor Sandy. God's presence is forever with me. Even in the worst nightmares of life I can feel His presence and His peace.

Camilia Kyle

He Comforts me.

REFLECTION

Although I am an adult I still am a wounded inner child that holds all the pain deep inside. It is the part of me I need to let go, I need to move beyond. It is a struggle because at times it provides cover for unhealthy behavior on my part. It is my crutch or excuse for why the abuse happened. My thinking needs to change.

1969 Paula

I met Paula Reynolds Wilkerson in 3rd grade at Sharpsburg Elementary School (Norwood, OH). While we both had the same last name "Reynolds" we were not related. When teachers assigned seats alphabetically we sat next to each other. The kids called us the "Reynolds Sisters." Paula is still my friend today. Best friends. She is the one who invited me to Sunday school. I think I started going with her when I was about 10. Paula's mom, Betty, would drive her five children to Sunday school and allowed each to bring a friend. Their old Pontiac car was so crowded I would sit on Paula's lap or she on mine; it was fun. At first I thought it would be a way of getting out of the house. Paula was my friend and it would be better than listening to Lily. But after a while I wanted to go; I needed to go. When Lily was slow to approve I would use Paula as my excuse: "If I don't go Paula will be all alone and bored to death." I think I went with her until I was about 13; it seemed to stop once Ted moved in.

I can remember the first time at Sunday school; it was amazing. The teacher talked about God and his Love, his unconditional love and his unconditional forgiveness. WOW!! Nothing I had ever done or could do would stop God from loving me, ME! I never heard this before. God died for me because he loved me and I was forgiven. This was confusing because I knew the teacher wasn't lying to me.

Lily at times would say she loved me but the hitting, the hurting, the name calling; the abuse to me was what I thought was love. Ed never expressed love but he was my dad. I was associating abuse with love and now I was being told there was another life. I was being told that love, true love was completely different. For me to go to Sunday school and hear about HIM, to hear that real love was pure and unconditional was like drinking a glass of cold water. I had never experienced love this way before. Now I knew that there was hope and I wanted more, much more.

REFLECTION

Attending bible school with Paula exposed a part of me I did not know I had. It awoke a necessary part of my identity, of who I am, it awoke my spirituality. I could not see it or feel it but I knew it was a much needed part. I did not understand it all at first but I was now aware of a God so loving, forgiving, and compassionate. In a relationship with God I could restore myself.

1970 Miss Wantuck

I WENT TO Sharpsburg Elementary School from Kindergarten through Eighth Grade. During all those years Lily never once attended a school event: PTO meetings, plays, conferences. The school was close by so she could walk and was not dependent on someone else for a ride; it didn't matter, she didn't come.

In Fourth Grade I had this great teacher, Miss Wantuck. She cared for us, her class, taught us that we were important, that who we are is important in life. She actually made house calls if the parent(s) missed a conference. That was when I heard her bragging to Lily how good a student I was. I felt "Wow! She likes me." After she left all Lily could say was "Wipe that grin off your face!"

1970 Phyllis

ONE DAY WHEN I was nine my neighbor and friend Phyllis (a year younger) and I decided to walk from Norwood to Deer Park to visit my sister Sissy and her husband Fred who had recently moved back after military service. We were gone all day and had a good time. Fred drove us the six miles home about dinner time. Phyllis' mom was upset as we did not ask permission to leave the neighborhood alone and we did not tell her where we were. Phyllis was grounded for two weeks!! Lily neither said nor did anything to me – no yelling, not anger, no punishment. I began to wonder: "What was the difference? Why was Phyllis grounded while I was not? Why was Phyllis' mom concerned while Lily was not?" There I was – no rules, no restrictions, and no answers.

REFLECTION

Phyllis' mom set boundaries, Lily did not. Boundaries provide space for me to be myself. They are a critical part of growing that I missed Knowing my rights in dealing with others, knowing what role I play and the respect I should receive from others, even knowing that I could say Yes or No, that I had the power to be myself were boundaries that I lacked which became clearer over time.

1970 Tuna

I HATE TUNA! I can't stand the smell of it or the taste of it. When you are a child you cannot stand up and defend yourself from abuse. You don't even know that it is abuse. You think everyone's home life is like yours. And if you want the verbal abuse, physical abuse, and sexual abuse to stop you certainly don't know how to do that. You can't do that.

But yet you carry the shame and the quilt of the abuse. You take ownership of it. For certainly there must have been something wrong with you to cause the abuse. I thought. "If I own it I have the power to change it." But it doesn't work that way; I was really powerless.

I remember once standing up to my mom in defiance. My mom probably had a little OCD. Her house was always extremely clean! Anytime, all the time. You didn't dare put your feet on the furniture or not use a coaster. When you finished your drink, you didn't leave the dirty glass in the sink. You wash it right away! If you accidentally spilled a drink or something you would get a spanking.

One day my mom made tuna on toast for dinner. It was warm tuna, mushroom soup, served on toast. I hated it! We sat down at the table and I refused to eat it. My mom demanded that I eat it. I said, "No!"

No one told Lily no! She grabbed my fork, put some tuna and toast on it and tried to force it in my mouth. I defiantly closed my mouth and held it shut. She grabbed my head, trying to force my mouth open. I tried shaking my head. Tuna was all in my hair!

I took off running with mom chasing me with that plate of tuna on toast in her hand. I ran into the living room, mom right behind me. I jumped up on the coffee table, jumped on the couch. Mom was right behind me! She jumped up on the couch right behind me! I yelled, "your feet are on the couch" That really made her mad. She slapped me!

I took off running again! Mom right behind me! She never could get a bite of that tuna on toast in my mouth. By the time the battle ended I had been slapped and whipped! I also had to clean up all the mess. There was tuna on toast everywhere! On me, on the couch, on the coffee table, on the floor, on the curtains, you name it. But none of it got in my mouth!

I counted it as one small victory for myself. I don't know if the whipping and the slap and certainly the mess was worth it, but victories (or what I perceived as a victory) for me didn't come often, so I still counted it as one.

REFLECTION

In defying Lily I was learning to be myself, I was letting my authentic-self speak. I allowed myself to know what I know and to feel what I was feeling —a great dislike of tuna. I may have picked the wrong time to defy her and certainly I paid the price. Sadly Lily could not be authentic herself and listen to what I was saying, to what I meant.

1970 Measles & Blindness

WHEN I WAS around nine years old I got a bad case of the measles. It was awful! It broke out all over my body and I was running a fever and sitting in a dark room alone. I don't know if it was an old saying or factual information, but my mom had heard that light could cause you to go blind if you had the measles. So all the blinds were drawn and the drapes were closed and no lamps were on.

I felt awful and I was in bed crying. Joy (my brother Kent's wife at the time) came into my room and put a cool rag on my forehead and gave me something cold to drink. She even pulled the shade up a little on the far side of the room. She sat down beside my bed and held my hand.

Then my mom came in. She told Joy in a very stern voice that she shouldn't baby me. That if she did I would only milk it for all it was worth and I would put on quite a pity party. I remember lying there thinking how I really did feel awful and how nice Joy's comfort was. Joy got up and left. Mom walked over to the shade and pulled it down! "Do you want to go blind?" she screamed. She left my room and loudly closed the door behind her.

I started crying. I started sobbing. I was scared. Had that little bit of light been enough to blind me? I certainly felt awful and I had made mom mad. I couldn't help myself, I was really crying now. I tried to call out for Joy to come back. I could hear mom arguing with Joy outside my bedroom door. "I told you that you would only make things worse by babying her," mom yelled. "Listen to her now." Mom opened my door and yelled for me to shut up! She slammed my door and I buried my head under my pillow and cried.

I think I remember that so well, because it was a time when another label had been branded on me. I was the drama queen, over reacting; my feelings were bad or not true. Today I find myself with a chronic illness and I fight the depression of it like a prize fighter in a ring! I don't want to feel the aggravation, the physical pain, the exhaustion.......... it is wrong to feel...........but wait those are old messages, old lies. It is okay for me to feel my emotions, to cry sometimes, to rest in my Savior's arms and then I can go on.

I can share all my feelings with my husband Jim and my daughter Danielle and my father God. Never do they accuse me of having a pity party. They listen and hold me until I am strong once again to continue and strive.

I have never understood that term pity party anyway. Does that mean you exaggerate your feelings so much to get pity and then everyone is gathering around you, pitying you? That sounds awful! How could that ever be confused for comfort? For certainly I don't remember a time where I ever had a pity party and anyone, especially family were gathered around me pitying me. I hate pity. I do however sometimes long for and need comforting, encouragement and love.

I am okay with saying that. There was a time when I wouldn't have been able to identify or ask for comfort or encouragement or love. I can now, with those who will freely give it to me when I need it. That is not pity that is love.

1971 Fireman

ONE DAY, MY younger brother Joe and I were riding our ten speed bikes up a hill when my brakes froze. I flew off the bike and landed on my face cutting my lip and busting a tooth. My lip was bleeding, it hurt and I was crying partially from the pain and partially from the fear of what Lily would do. Lily was furious but didn't know whether to take me to the emergency room or not. Finally she decided to take me to the local firehouse which meant she had to ask a neighbor for a ride. This whole time I did not stop crying. Lily said I was over dramatic and slapped me. When we got to the firehouse things were different. The fireman was kind and said I was "a brave little girl." He cleaned the cut and treated it. But he could not save the tooth. I had to get a root canal as the nerve died. So much for being Lily's "most dramatic kid." I stopped crying because the fireman showed care, gentleness and understanding which were not what I received from Lily and my family.

REFLECTION

Once again the difference in how adults handle a situation became apparent. Lily was not comforting but the fireman was. Lily was annoyed while the fireman went about the task of cleaning the wound and calming me. How those around me reacted to my experiences taught me whom I could trust, whom I could go to in time of need and who empowered me or left me powerless. A child learns early on which parent is able to handle situations in a positive and healthy way and which parent cannot. With both of mine failing, my physical, mental and spiritual health would be greatly impacted.

1972 Lily

THINGS WERE NEVER good between my mother and me. I mean, there were times when we did have good moments. What I mean is that she always took her anger and frustration out on me and always seemed to be greatly disappointed in me while I was a child, but there were those moments when she was tender and funny. I worship those memories. They weren't often. My mom just didn't get along with her daughters.

The fondest memories that I have from my childhood of my mom is that she would take a napkin or paper towel and fold it some way and make a nurse's hat out of it for me and pin it on my head and I would play nurse with my doll (back then nurse's wore those white hats). Also she could play jacks! WOW! I don't know how she learned to be so good, but she would throw that rubber ball up and could catch 10 or more jacks at a time. I loved to watch her. Other times she didn't know I was there or if she noticed me it was in very negative ways.

I remember once, I was about 11 or 12 years old. We had gotten back from the grocery store (don't remember who took us or how we got there because mom didn't drive) but she and I were putting groceries away in the kitchen. There was a knock at the front door and I left the kitchen to go answer it. My friend was at the door and wanted me to come outside. I must have stayed at the door talking too long or something because the next thing I knew mom was standing in the little archway between the kitchen and the living room and she threw a 5lb bag of flour at me. The bag hit the floor at my feet, flour went everywhere. I was so embarrassed to have my friend witness this. I turned around and mom said, "You are supposed to be putting the groceries away." I told my friend I couldn't come outside, closed the door and I remember having to clean the flour up.

1972 Kent

I AM ABOUT 11 years old. I have been going to Sunday school with my friend Paula. I have learned that Jesus loves me and that He loves me unconditionally. He died for me. I am so excited. I want to tell the world!

I have a kick ball. I take my pen and write in carefully artistic print on my ball......"Jesus Saves" ...."Jesus Loves You".......I draw little flowers and smiley faces on it. It looks so pretty when I am finished.

The ball is lying on the floor in the living room where I left it after I finished making it so beautiful. My oldest brother comes in. He is almost 15 years older than me. He picks up the ball and looks at it. "Who did this?" he asked.

"I did." I answered. I am sure he is going to compliment my art work and writings that I did on the ball. "Who told you this crap? He asks. "This is bullshit." I stand there confused, hurt."What does this mean? Jesus saves? He asks.

I try to explain. "Jesus saves us from our sins. He forgives us." I am almost crying and I am about eleven years old trying to explain to a 25 or 26 year old man.

"What is a sin?" he asks, his voice getting louder. "If I say the word shit, it that a sin?" I think so; I know you aren't supposed to say bad words. I nod yes. "That is crazy!" he yells. How can a word send you to hell? Tears are coming full force now. I shrug my shoulders in an answer. He throws the ball down.

I don't remember what happen to that ball after that. I don't remembering that I ever saw it again. I do remember sitting in my room after that, crying and feeling like I had disappointed my brother and Jesus. I wanted my big brother to brag on my great art work that I as a child had so carefully created on my ball. I longed for a compliment.

I wish I had been able to explain things better to my brother. I knew God loved me, I knew Jesus loved me.........but what my brother said confused me. I wish I was wise like my Sunday school teacher.........but I was only 11 years old. Maybe I couldn't explain it, but I would still believe. I just tried really hard after that to keep it to myself.

1973 Cindy & Brian

WHEN I WAS in 7th grade, 12 years old, I rode to school with our next door neighbor Cindy and her mom. Cindy was a year or two older than me. She was dating a guy name Brian. He had been in and out of juvenile detention and he was now 18. I think he was on probation at the time. All the guys we hung around with were 17 and 18 years old or older. A lot of them had been in trouble as a juvenile for stealing. They drank a lot.

We get to middle school and Cindy's mom drops us off in front of the school. Cindy stops walking toward the school as soon as her mom pulls away. She turns toward me and says, "we are skipping school today."

I am surprised but I do what I am told. We walk about a block and Billy and Brian are waiting in a car. We drive to this other guy's house. His parents are at work. The guys are already drinking. They want to play strip poker. I don't want to play. Cindy starts laughing and calling me chicken. Then one of the guys is holding me down and I am crying and fighting. Brian is taking off my pants. I am on my period and have a pad on.

"Gross," Brian screams and gets off of me. The other guys turn away. I put on my pants still crying. Thank God, I was on my period or I would have been gang raped. I know that was their intention. I curl up in a corner so embarrassed. Cindy parties with them. She gets naked and has intercourse with Brain. Everyone parties while I just sit in the corner, too afraid to move.

Billy drops Cindy and me off at the school yard just before school lets out. Cindy tells me to keep my big mouth shut!

I do.

REFLECTION

I could sense that the dysfunction was all around me. I read once that "hurt people hurt people." I think there is some truth to that statement and it is why it is so important to get help, so important to heal, and so important to be around safe people. I needed safe people who would treat me with respect and who would not take advantage of me. Safe people who would listen to me without being judgmental and help me understand what was happening.

1973 Betty

So let me say this. I got saved when I was 12 years old. This means that a Sunday school teacher told me about a loving God who gave His son for me. She taught me about genuine, real love. There was nothing I could do to earn this love, it was a gift. Unconditionally, I believed it and received it. I was a 12 year old child who truly trusted her heavenly Father then and NOW!

I wanted to be baptized and back then a minor had to have a parent's consent. When I came home from church and told my mom I had gotten saved and wanted to get baptized, she said no. She said "You have to be perfect to be baptized and you are nowhere near perfect!" She said that I wasn't good enough to be a Christian because I did not live it, wasn't pure. Lily absolutely refused to sign the permission form. As a child I got the message from my mom that I wasn't good enough, a failure, who was never going to be good enough for God or anyone.

The following Sunday as I was getting into the car Paula's mom, Betty, asked if I had my signed consent form. Betty could not image why a mom "wouldn't want her kids baptized. It's a good thing." So I received the message in my heart and soul that I would never be good enough!

REFLECTION

For the rest of my life I have never felt "good enough." The more we feel something the more we believe it. It becomes part of our internal beliefs. There is no pill that can cure me of this stinking thinking. I'm finished with that negative thinking! These thoughts, these lies, hindered my growth and I refuse to allow them to affect me anymore! I need to change my beliefs about myself.

1974 Chuck

───── ∿∿ ─────

MANY YEARS LATER my mom and dad would divorce and my dad would remarry. He and his new wife, Barb, had a son, Chuck. People say my dad changed. That he stopped drinking. He did start going to church while he was living in Kentucky. That he wasn't violent and yet, Barb divorced and remarried my dad three times!

While writing this book I called my half-brother and step mom to ask about dad. I wanted to know if dad had really changed before his death. My half-brother was very open about the severe whippings he received as a child. They were excessive, abusive. They didn't stop until my half-brother was in his late teens and he was big enough to stand up to my dad. He also spoke of dad's temper - throwing plates of food, beating dogs with chains and hitting my step mom.

I am sure as my dad got older he did mellow. You can't be as forceful when your strength is gone. A lot of people saw my father as kind and a nice man. But I have never heard that description from anyone who had to live with him. I can only hope that in the latter part of his life he did accept God's amazing love and forgiveness and truly became whole and healed from all the strongholds of brokenness he carried.

I have said it before and I will say it again. Healing is a process. The minute Jesus comes into your life you have forgiveness and love. If you have been a victim of abuse, you need to be purged from all the lies, brokenness, fear, etc. You grow in your walk with Christ and you grow in healing. The victim has to do the work. The good news is that Christ is right there with you. Leading, guiding, comforting, loving, healing, encouraging. He works in amazing ways.

REFLECTION

God's power is that He heals me through my relationship with Him. We carry the load together and if I stumble He carries more of the load until I recover. We become partners in restoring me to what He created me to be. Some have told me that I should leave it all at the foot of the cross. But I can't leave my feelings, my emotions, my memories and my experiences, as horrible as they might be, because that would be leaving parts of me, parts of who I am, parts that are natural and important to my being; I would be incomplete. Rather I met Jesus at the foot of the cross and together we have partnered to carry my load.

1975 Ted

THERE CAME A time, I am not sure at what age it started, when all the neighborhood girls hung out with the older boys. I just remember that at 13 it was normal to be hanging with the 17 and 18 year old boys. One day Billy, one of the older neighbor boys, asked if I would like to go for a drive to visit one of his friends who was in Longview State Mental Hospital. Lily said it was OK so I went. Ted was 19 years old and I am not sure why he was in Longview, but after he got out he started to come to the neighborhood and visit. Lily, for whatever reason, allowed him to move in with us. Then the grooming started.

Ted became the predator. He would tell me I was beautiful, that he loved me, that we would be married someday. When he would sneak into my bedroom at night he would say that what we were doing was okay because we would get married but not to tell anyone. I didn't tell and so I ended up lying to Lily and my family. But this was love, Ted told me so and for once someone loved me. One time, Lily caught him in my bedroom in his shorts and accepted our excuse of falling asleep watching television.

When I was 14 I missed my period and didn't know what was happening. By the time I told my sister-in-law Teri (Kent's second wife) I was five months pregnant. She helped me tell Lily and that is when all hell broke loose. Ted split and left me on my own. After Lily found out I was pregnant, things turned so much worse! Her rage and abuse was worse than ever before. She called me all kinds of names. She called me liar and said I was nothing but a big fat liar (because I had lied to her when asked if anything was going on when she caught Ted in my bed) and she called me a whore. She told me I was over sexed! I didn't have a clue what she meant. But then she would say that some people just can't help themselves that they have to have sex all the time and I was one of those people. I was 14 years old and had just been molested by an older man and naïve about so much, but this was what she was yelling at me.

She said that I might need help and then said she could put me away or make me go away and get help if she wanted to. She slapped me and cried. I knew I had hurt her, but honestly I was such a confused child that I didn't mean to hurt anyone! I blamed myself for the molestation, for getting pregnant. It wasn't until years, years later through counseling that I began to learn that I was a young girl manipulated by an older man who just wanted to have sex with a 13 year old! To this day I still feel shame and I constantly work on not blaming myself completely. I work at giving some of the blame to the guy who used me and to my parents who didn't protect me. I try to balance that with a forgiveness that sets me free and is taught by Christ. I don't want to live in those chains anymore and hating them doesn't hurt them, it wrecks me and makes me bitter, so there is no use in it.

Right after my mom found out I was pregnant and she threatened Ted with statutory rape charges (she never had any intentions on charging him, if she did then child services would find out he lived with us and that she allowed the dating). She said that to make him leave but Ted began calling. When I would answer the phone he would talk, when anyone else answered he would hang up. I didn't get to answer the phone very often but once I did and Ted spoke rapidly, he told me that I should write him letters telling him what was going on and he would write back and to leave them under the front door mat. I was to ask if I could get the mail out of the mailbox in the morning and leave the letters under the mat and he would leave his there.

Man was I one confused, hurt, messed up young girl! My mom was abusing me, some guy was harassing me after molesting me and he was talking all kinds of stuff and I just didn't understand anything that had happened or was happening or where to run. When I look back now, I cry for that little girl. I cry because honestly all she wanted was to be loved and she would have done anything for love and I guess she did.

Was she powerless? I don't know. I have professionals telling me to look at the facts and see the

Mike Rogers

LOVING ME

abuse, maybe I thought if I carried all the blame all these years I could protect a mom I so wanted to be loved and accepted by.

Anyway Ted left a note and I don't remember what all I wrote, mostly that mom was going crazy, that she said I had to give the baby up for adoption, no choice, and that I was scared. The note passing didn't last long. Somehow mom found out and I was once again labeled a liar and untrustworthy. My mother always yelled at me that I couldn't be trusted. From the moment she found out that I was pregnant until the day she died her labels for me were: I was a liar and couldn't be trusted. I believed those lies for many, many, years. I think I will always have to work on healing and believing good about myself and self-worth. The lies were instilled in me. That is what abusive words do. They cut into your heart and leave a scar there and the victim of those words begins to believe everything awful that was said about her.

Yes, I lied when asked what Ted was doing in my bed. Yes I snuck letters and put them under the mat. I was so young, so scared, so confused and I honestly thought that if I loved this guy I should let him do anything he wanted to me. After all, isn't that what I had seen and learned as a child? Didn't my dad do whatever he wanted to my mom? Didn't Oscar use her too?

Now they (my mom and my oldest brother) were saying I had to give my baby away. I understand more now and I am so thankful that I did give Beth up for adoption. If I had kept her, she wouldn't have had the life and opportunities that she did have. She was given a life and parents that loved her. What an amazing gift. But at the time, I knew that I only had a short time to tell this baby everything, so in the quiet of the night I would lay on my bed with my hand on my stomach and talk to Beth who laid inside my womb.

REFLECTION

When I think about these times I get physically nauseated. I hate, hate, hate that this happened. It was the most frightening and painful time in my life.

Promises were used by the perpetrator to get me to comply, to go along. I was a hostage of my needs which he played upon. In my compliance I assumed some responsibility of the statutory rape. I was the victim but trying to manage the situation to keep the peace I made the situation worse. I had to tell Lily but I knew she could not handle it and I feared her reaction.

Victims become stuck and wrapped up in the shame, always the shame and it's always the same. It continues to exist just the same as Pat Conroy in *The Death of Santini* writes:

> *I could have used a thousand scenes from my childhood, but the theme was always humiliation and a shame that could never be removed or washed away. It's that indelible shame I feel today as I write some of the same words I wrote more than thirty-six years ago. The fear is the same —the self-loathing, the suicide wishes the same—the waking up screaming in the middle of the night will always be the same.*

1976 Beth

MY MOM CALLED my school and had a talk with the principal. Since it was now early March and the baby was due in June, he agreed to let me stay home from school and have my school work sent home to me. I don't know what she said to him but, he was a very kind man and he wanted me to be able to finish the year out.

My mom told my friends that I had moved to Kentucky to live with my dad. My best friend Paula was given my Aunt Sarah's address in Lexington, Ky., and told that was my address where I was living. Paula would write me letters and mail them to my aunt's house thinking I lived there. My aunt would then mail them to my house. My mom would read them to make sure I wasn't telling Paula anything about the truth and then I got to read the letter. I would answer Paula's letter and give it to mom. Mom would read my letter and send it to Aunt Sarah's house (so it would have a Kentucky postmark) and then Aunt Sarah would forward it to Paula. That is the only friend I had contact with and Paula did not know I was really at home in Norwood, locked up in the attic, not able to go out.

June 1st 1976 came and I began having bad back pain and it got worse as time went on. Mom knew it was labor and called Joy my brother Kent's first wife. She drove my mom, Sissy and me to the hospital. Mom asked the doctor not to let me see the baby. She told me it would be easier that way. In the labor room, I remember hearing her cry and heard them say it was a girl. But they refused to let me see her. They rushed her out of the room. When I was taken to my hospital room, I was not on the maternity floor. Mom had told the doctor that if I saw other babies it would be too hard on me. The sooner I forgot this, the better! So that was the beginning of the plan. We would pretend that this never happened and that I was to go back to school in the fall like nothing happened and I was never to talk about this again.

My mom didn't come in and visit me while I was in the labor room. Sissy came back once and squeezed my hand and then left. The nurses would rub my back and talk to me as I laid there crying and in pain.

My mom didn't visit me in my hospital room after I had the baby. Joy did and told me that Lily was in the hospital's waiting room but would not come in. Then Joy gave me an orange dog stuffed animal. But she told me, that mom didn't like that she bought it for me because she didn't want me to think I was getting rewarded for what I had done and put everyone through. I promised Joy that I wouldn't think of it as a reward. After she left, I held that stuffed dog and cried. I kept that dog until the day I would meet Beth, my daughter in person some 18 years later. Then I gave it to Beth.

I was dismissed a couple days later. The nurse was wheeling me out to Joy's car where she and my mom waited. I remember the nurse telling me that I was very brave for a 15 year old girl. I didn't exactly know what she meant by that. I had done exactly what I was instructed to do and I didn't argue about it. I didn't feel brave at all because on the inside I had a million questions with no one to turn to for answers.

As soon as I got home from the hospital, my mom said that we would never talk about any of this again. She looked at me and said why don't you call your friend Paula tell her you are back home to live and see if she wants to go do something with you? Just like that it was to be erased! We never again talked about the statutory rape or Beth or my life or if I was okay or if I was coping. She never asked and she just couldn't care about me.

I did call Paula. I had just given birth so there wasn't a lot I could do. She walked over and together Paula and I walked down to Water Works Park. It was where a lot of the teens hung out. It had a public pool and everyone swam there. I told Paula I didn't feel like swimming because I was on my period. We just talked and got caught up. But I never confided in Paula, I was afraid if she found out what Lily would do and I did not want to lose Paula as a friend; even now she is my closest friend. My mom said to never tell anyone and then she kept bad mouthing me. I was embarrassed, confused and really messed up. Paula had signed up for the Norwood Indianettes at the end of the year. It was like a cheering group of flag girls. I was soon to find out that I didn't fit in anywhere when I went back to school. It was a nightmare of fear, accusations and bullying.

When I went back to school in the fall Paula had a new group of friends that were all in the flag group. (We were still friends, but we didn't see each other as often) Rumors had circulated that I had gotten pregnant. Ted, Beth's father had decided to tell everyone he knew that I was pregnant. Soon it spread like wild fire. But my mom said, no matter what deny it. So I did. Again and again, I would argue with teens from school that I had not been pregnant. The word "slut" was written on my locker. It was 1976 and things were a little different back then. I would sit down at my school desks and find nasty drawings and words written on them.

Some guys would ask me out after hearing the rumors and presuming I was easy only to find out that I wasn't and they didn't get lucky. Much later, there was one guy named Tony who asked me out and we started going steady. It wasn't a good relationship. He was trying to have sex with me and after what I had been through I wasn't letting any guy near me. I thought he cared, but he was hoping I would evidently give in and when I didn't he dropped me for another girl.

REFLECTION

When I look back on this now I don't know how I survived. The teasing and the treatment I got when I went back to school were TERRIBLE!!! I felt dirty and so awful plus I was grieving over everything that had happened. I wanted to pretend that the molestation never happened, that there was no statutory rape, the abuse didn't happen, but it did! It makes me sick thinking about it. To survive I disassociated myself many times. Years later I leaned that this is often a mechanism that abused children use to survive.

I am a victim in a culture that does not like the word. Lily and others held me more responsible for the rape than they did Ted, the perpetrator. You can count the times when talking about rape that you have heard comments like "She asked for it" or "Look at how she dresses." In the process they absolve the perpetrator of any responsibility for his actions. When Lily told me to forget it ever happened, to move on, she denied the reality of what happened – her daughter was a victim of rape. She tried to cover over the experience and all the emotions and feelings I had because of the rape. She reinforced or rather increased the severity of the traumatic impact because she, herself, could not face its reality. Such denial fostered confusion on my part as well as a loss of personal value (I became "less than"). It attacked my belief systems, my self-respect, my ability to trust others, to feel safe, and to be intimate. My needs became less important than the needs and urges of the perpetrator. He continued to live his life unaffected while I was made to take the blame. Many confused my image for my identity. They saw or were told things about me that gave them a very superficial image of me but it wasn't me. My identity, my core beliefs, my values and virtues found deep inside me make me who I am and they were under attack.

I built walls to protect from the pain and abuse, built a shell around my life, I hardened myself. In the process I let myself be identified by the statutory rape, by the abuse and trauma. There are many today who think of a survivor as one who has lived through a trauma but is still wrapped up by the impact of the abuse, of the trauma. But I can't live like that because it stops me from growing, from being the person God created me to be, my authentic self. Just as in Deuteronomy 32:13 these hardened lives, these rocks and stones are turned into oil and honey through the love of Jesus Christ.

1976 BIBLE

My first real job was as a clerk for the Norwood Board of Education. I mostly filed and occasionally answered the phones like during lunch. With some of my pay I bought my own Bible. I would read it, memorizing verses and following my old Sunday school notes. I was really curious of Jesus and why He loved me so I spent a lot of time reading the New Testament.

REFLECTION

Individually we are created with specific talents, strengths, creative instincts. One person may be good in sports while another excels in math. Parents have the primary responsibility to nurture and provide space for these characteristics to grow and develop. I found my curiosity on fire with a search for God and His Truth but not because of my family's help. It grew out of the confusion in my life and the dissonance for what I felt deep inside and what I saw around me. My "wounded Inner child" was reaching out for help and the Word seemed to be the Way.

1978 Steve

AT THE END of my junior year I met Steve. He was two years older and out of school. I met him through a friend and we started dating. He was good looking, had a job and an apartment and threw a bunch of parties. I would go to the parties but I never drank or smoked pot. I was afraid I would turn out like my dad, the fear of being an abusive addict like him kept me straight and I have never touched drugs or alcohol. I can at least thank him for giving me that fear!

My home life was awful. Mom and I fought all the time. I could never do anything right. Now she could abuse me with even more words. I was the slut, the girl who broke her trust, she would slap me and call me names, throw things and many times I would just sit in my room and cry.

We never talked about the statutory rape or the baby or my life or if I was okay or if I was coping, she never asked and she just couldn't care about me. At school during study hall or break I would use the telephone in the hall and call the Children's Home and ask about the baby. They weren't allowed to tell me much. Just that she had been adopted and that the adoptive mother was a school teacher and that she had a 3 year old brother who was also adopted. They told me to move on, but no one ever told me how I was supposed to do that!

March 17, 1979 I turned 18 years old. I was a senior in high school and I made fairly good grades in spite of it all. I loved to read and I read everything I could get my hands on. I had been dating Steve for a while and when he asked me to move in with him I said no. I didn't want people to think I was a slut like all the rumors that went around said. I didn't feel like a slut. I had certainly NOT enjoyed sex when I was being abused. I just had laid there waiting for it to be over. So anyway Steve said we should get married then. So one week after my 18th birthday while I was still a senior in high school I got married. My mom didn't try to talk me out of it at all. I think she was glad I would be gone.

Soon after I was married to Steve I found out that Steve liked to do drugs a lot, and he liked to sell drugs and buy drugs and he liked to drink a lot and party. I don't know how he kept his job, but he did. It was so hard getting up and going to school because Steve would have people in and out of our 2 room apartment all the time at all hours. Weekends were crazy! I would come home from school or my part time job and Steve would have pounds of marijuana laid out on the table, weighing it and putting it in baggies. There would be pills in the refrigerator that he popped like candy. In spite of the constant partying that was going on, I stayed in school and graduated. I was the first one in my immediate family to ever graduate high school. My parents hadn't, my older siblings hadn't and I was so proud of myself.

The day of graduation came. As I drove us to the ceremony Steve drank during the entire ride. I received my diploma. After everything that had happened to me and everything that I had gone through, I managed to graduate and with good grades. After the ceremony my fellow classmates threw their caps up in the air and all their parents and family ran down to where we all were standing. I stood there and looked around. I saw no one. Not my mom, not my siblings, not even Steve. I stood there for a few minutes and waited and waited. I had sent everyone an invitation to my graduation. I had sent them to my parents, my siblings, my aunts and uncles. I didn't see anyone.

I found Steve half passed out in the auditorium seats. I managed to get him into my car. I drove to our apartment and called my mom. I ask her why she hadn't come to my graduation. She said she did come that she had been there. I didn't have the typical graduation party that graduating seniors have: no cake, no cards, no celebration, no hugs, and no congratulations. I don't know if my mom was at the ceremony or not. I never asked her again. If she was, she didn't address me or hug me afterwards and she didn't congratulate me. I know my older sister or brother wasn't there. I asked her why she didn't have a cake or family over to celebrate for me and she said that I was married and that I was Steve's problem now. It wasn't her responsibility to have a celebration. That was it. I remember crying so hard after I got off the phone. Steve was passed out and I was alone on my graduation day.

Steve got worse. It took stronger and more drugs to get him high. I was working and still hadn't even tried any kind of drug or alcohol. I saw my dad in Steve and the effects of his addiction, it didn't look like fun to me and I certainly didn't want to be an addict.

Steve was a very nice guy but this nice guy had a bad drug and alcohol problem. We separated and got back together several times. Had arguments when he was high and I would leave. Once I left and went to my sister's to stay. She had an apartment in Norwood.

My mom and I were barely speaking, we just argued all the time. She adored Steve and wasn't too interested in hearing how bad his habits were becoming. When I told her about the sexually transmitted disease he had caught, she said that my dad had brought them home before and that it wasn't anything to leave Steve over.

My sister and mom were arguing at the time too, I don't remember why. My mom's anger was always directed at my sister and me. Anyway I was staying at my sister's apartment because I had left Steve. Steve had hooked up with some female (I think she was a hooker) and gotten crabs (sexually transmitted disease) and I freaked out! It was disgusting and I was very upset. Steve's excuse was that he was stoned at the time and didn't know what he was doing. I needed a break.

Ted (the predator) had been trying to contact me through friends. He said he had to talk to me. I called him. (I was still a very insecure, frightened young lady and I certainly hadn't learned anything about relationships yet.) He told me that if I gave him all the information about the baby he could get her back for me. (LIES) He was manipulating me. He had since married and had a child or children and said he was separated from his wife.

I was a terribly confused young lady. Everything that had happened had not been talked about or explained. I hadn't had any counseling and was taught to pretend the statutory rape, the pregnancy, the abuse and everything hadn't happen. I certainly didn't know how dysfunctional everything had been and I had never been taught anything about typical (normal) life relationships or families.

I was so very naïve. I told Ted everything I knew about the adoption which wasn't much: that the baby was a girl, when she was born and what adoption home we used. He assured me that what had happen to me hadn't been wrong or bad and that I just had to believe him. He persuaded me to let him use me once more. That night my younger brother called from a local bowling alley. Ted was up there bowling with his wife! I had been used again.

I went back to Steve several days later. When he was sober and not using he was very nice but the problem was those straight times were becoming fewer and farther between. But still we stayed together. About a year later Steve and I had invited some friends over. Steve wanted to turn it into a party. He had begun drinking and smoking pot way before anyone showed up. I didn't know it, but he had taken some other drugs. Pills I think. Not sure.

After our friends arrived, I noticed that Steve was getting really stoned and acting more weird than ever. My friend Betty was trying to talk to me and Steve had started hallucinating. He started yelling at Betty to get away from his wife. He then started yelling all kinds of crazy things and kicked over the coffee table. He was knocking pictures off the walls and breaking things and screaming! We had a 25 or 50 gallon aquarium and he knocked it over. Water and fish went everywhere!

Thinking she was a guy, he swung at Betty, he certainly didn't recognize her, and just missed hitting her. Betty's husband was trying to calm Steve down and our friend Willie was trying to restrain Steve. Steve was out of his mind! He lunged toward me and began choking me. He had both hands around my neck and I was clawing and pulling his arms and trying to get his hands off from around my neck. Willie was literally on his back trying to get him off of me. Tony and Betty were trying to help me. Someone called the police. I was on the ground kicking and trying to breathe.

The cops busted through the front door after hearing the screaming and the noise. Six police men were now on Steve and I was underneath it all! By the time they got Steve off of me I had passed out. I woke up in the hospital and found out that Steve was in the psychiatric ward in the hospital. Whatever he had taken had completely caused severe hallucinations. He had fought the police and didn't know who they were, was seeing crazy things and now was locked up in the hospital.

I was going to be okay physically. I had several bruises on my body and bruises around my neck. I was sore and my voice was hoarse and weak. My friend picked me up from the hospital. We went back to the house that Steve and I were renting. I walked inside. It looked like a bomb had gone off! Broken furniture everywhere, overturned plants and broken pictures, a broken aquarium and water and dead fish everywhere. Curtains were down. It didn't seem possible that one man could have done all this, but some drugs can make a person super strong and friends just couldn't get Steve down. I started to sob. I just fell on the floor and sobbed! I didn't have the physical strength to start cleaning the mess. I didn't have the resources to leave. I was sore and scared and alone and my throat was hurting, my neck hurt, my whole body ached and emotionally I was a wreck. My friend left and I went upstairs and cried myself to sleep on the bed.

I found out that Steve was still committed either in the psychiatric ward or drug rehabilitation unit or maybe it was one in the same. I hadn't spoken to him. Someone gave me the update. They said, that Steve didn't remember anything that he had done. Nothing! When he heard it, he had trouble believing it. He had never been violent toward me before. He had never broken things before. Usually he had just passed out after getting high or drunk. He had a long way to go toward rehabilitating. I knew that we would never get back together. I could have been killed. I had had enough. I just felt like a walking zombie.

Some friends had offered to help clean up the place. The wooden floor had a permanently warped section in it now because of all the water that spilled and had stayed on the floor. They picked up most of the stuff. I had trouble staying at the house. I was afraid that Steve would get out and be crazy again. When I did sleep I had terrible nightmares. I had to move out. Steve was going to be away for a while and I had made up my mind we were splitting up. I couldn't afford to rent the house on my own. I had a lot to face and I felt so very alone.

REFLECTION

I can't read this today without getting sick. Physically I feel my body reacting and I pull back. I was so confused, so broken and the people in my life were broken. I wish I could say it never happened but it did. I feel so sad for that 18 year old girl (me) who wanted her parents, her family to be proud of her. She felt like such a failure then, how badly she wanted their forgiveness, love, and acceptance. I have it now through the love of Christ. His love for me is my identity. Good News – Yesterday is gone. Today – I stand a new woman.

I have learned in therapy that the most important step in healing is accepting that I was a victim, The Victim. The shame and guilt that I carry must give way to the secret that the abuse did happen and it was not my fault. My dysfunctional life is driven by the impact of the trauma of the abuse and hiding all of it welled up deep inside me.

1979 Ed

MY DAD REMARRIES. Actually he married and divorced Barb three times.

1983 Tony

I DON'T WANT to write about Abe's biological father. I don't want to write about how many times I have been married or my teen pregnancy. I don't want to admit the mistakes I have made, the hurt I have caused. I don't want to admit the ugliness of my yesterdays. I don't want to look at the abuse! It is ugly! It is painful! But this is part of my healing...

Shame! Shame is the thing I fight the most, it is my constant struggle. I am so ashamed and so embarrassed. But there comes a time in healing when you look at the whole story. You really do have to forgive those who have hurt you and you really do have to ask forgiveness for those you have hurt.

I have been deeply hurt. I have deeply hurt others. I could give you a thousand reasons why I did what I did. Why I made the choices I made. You can read the cause and effect in this book, you can see the rippling cycle that continues until healing is sought, but the facts remain. Our choices affect others...for the good or for the bad.

I am working on forgiving myself. I am working on loving myself. I am working on seeing myself through the eyes of God. It is a process. Sometimes I do better at it than other times. Sometimes I really suck at it. But I press on.

I am deeply ashamed and embarrassed that my three children all have different biological fathers. They have had a steady, Christian father who loves them in their life for the past 23 years, my husband Jim. In writing this book I have to be vulnerable, I have to be honest. I understand why I did what I did at those times, but that doesn't make it right.

When I was a sophomore in high school I met Tony who was also a sophomore. He was popular and nice and funny and we started dating. He had heard the rumors about me and probably felt that I would be easy. I wasn't. At the time I didn't want to ever have sex again! I associated sex with abuse and heartache. He eventually dumped me for another girl.

I married my first husband Steve in March of 1979 while a senior in high school. We separated around Feb. of 1982. I was out at a store one day and ran into Tony. We hadn't seen each other since my sophomore year in high school. We went out on a couple of dates. I spent the night with him. I missed my period the next month. I wasn't sure if Steve was the father or Tony. I was ashamed. I thought Steve was probably Abe's dad because I had only slept with Tony once. But once is all it takes.

16 years later Abe wanted to know who his biological father was. (I had been honest with him about not knowing for sure) We had blood work from Steve and Tony done. Tony was his father. For a very short time Tony saw Abe. But Tony wasn't too interested in being his father or having a relationship with Abe. In my opinion he was just too selfish for that. I know that hurt Abe a lot. Abe and I have talked about it. Tony had the problem, not Abe. Tony was stupid enough to be given a very special son and then walk out on him.

I am deeply sorry that I put my son in that situation. I am deeply sorry that I had relationships with men who were not healthy enough themselves to value a woman or the child. I was confused and messed up emotionally, I didn't know how to identify a healthy man emotionally and I certainly wasn't able to have a healthy relationship. Healing would come many years later.

My kids are amazing. Generational curses have been broken. The chains are gone. Abe, Jack and Danielle are believers, they love the

Lord. Abe has a wonderful Christian wife and they are expecting their first child this September. They have been married 7 years. Jack was in the Marines for five years and held the rank of Corporal. He is out now, working hard and living on his own. Danielle is 17 years old a senior in high school this year, straight A student, identified as gifted. All three love the Lord and have grown into remarkable individuals.

Jim and I through God's amazing love and grace are so blessed. Many people reading this will be shocked to learn my background. I am a new woman. God makes all things new!

REFLECTION

Shame has been my companion for too many years. I get stuck and struggle to move forward. I am reminded of a quote from Joyce Meyer *The thoughts you have about yourself can be power draining or power building.* I pray every day to be power building.

Each bad relationship, each abuse by Ed and also by Lily reinforced the negative I was told and felt about myself. In time it became my core beliefs, it became my identity; it was who I am – liar, bad, guilty, shameful. With such a belief structure in place each new relationship; each new situation was a repeat of my past because that was me and so I could do nothing else. I knew I needed to be different but I didn't know how.

1983 Ryan

I MET RYAN and we began to date. After all I had been through I knew that I did not want to get married. But when he asked I decided to move in with him. Lily was upset and berated me for not being married. She said it did not look good to be living with a man out of wedlock. We married but shortly afterwards I realized I did not want to be married to him. This was another mistake in a long line of mistakes in my shameful life.

1986 Linda M

SOMETIMES GOD PUTS people in your life for a reason that you may not know at the time; I call them "God People." Such is the case with Linda M. for whom I babysat. Linda had two children- a boy and a girl- and needed to work as she was a single parent. The kids spent many over-nights at my house. Eventually Linda got back on her feet and became a successful business professional. One day as she was picking up her kids she turned to me and said "I owe you!" She paid me back by sav-ing my life. She supported me, helped me find a place to live and was there for me when I needed it the most. Linda is another example of a Loving God sending help in the form of others.

1986 Gus

I THEN MARRIED Gus (Jack's father); it was 1986. Abe was 4 years old (Tony, his biological father, was not in his life). Gus was my friend's brother. That is how I met him. He was good to Abe at the time. Jack was born in 1987. I loved being Jack and Abe's mother from the minute they were born. I cherished them.

Gus ended up hurting his back lifting something. He had back surgery and ended up getting hooked on the pain pills. He had terrible mood swings. I remember one day when Jack was just a baby not able to walk Gus had a doctor's appointment. It was a very hot summer day. I went with Gus to the doctor and we had the boys with us. Gus's back was really hurting that day and he had taken some pain pills. He was in a bad mood. I wanted to drive home because I was concerned with him driving under the influence of so many pain pills. He wouldn't let me drive. I didn't want the boys to be in the car with him driving. He took off and left me standing in the parking lot holding Jack on my hip and holding Abe's small hand. I had no money on me. There were no cell phones back then. It was very hot outside. I walked to a convenient store across the street. I called my mom collect from a phone booth. My brother ended up coming to pick me up. I stood in that convenient store with Jack on my hip and small Abe by my side for nearly an hour waiting for a ride. Gus never came back to check on us. That was just one of the incidents that happened.

1991 Gus

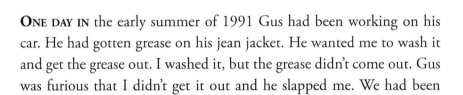

ONE DAY IN the early summer of 1991 Gus had been working on his car. He had gotten grease on his jean jacket. He wanted me to wash it and get the grease out. I washed it, but the grease didn't come out. Gus was furious that I didn't get it out and he slapped me. We had been having terrible arguments frequently and they were getting worse. The pain medicine he was taking made him have bad mood swings.

I left Gus and took Abe and Jack and went to my mom's. I don't like thinking about this time of my life and I don't like writing about it. I had been through a lot of terrible situations up until now, but the separation from Gus and divorce is probably one of the most painful because my sons were hurt during that time. Looking back I wish I had done things differently. I wish I had been wiser, stronger, smarter whatever it was needed to change what happened, but I can't change what happened. I can't fix all the bad choices that I have made or wrong that was done to me. I am learning how to forgive myself and others. Some days I do better than others.

Gus was furious that I left him. I had gotten a job at a retail store and he would come up to the parking lot and steal my car out of the parking lot. He had his own keys. I would get off work and go out to the parking lot to find my car was missing. Gus had taken it. I would call the police, and a police officer would tell me that my car was in Gus's driveway. The officer also told me that there was nothing I could do because Gus and I were still legally married.

Gus would call up the store screaming and yelling at the manager trying to get me fired. He came up to the store on my day off and told my manager that if he caught me with another man, he would shoot the man and me. All of that was just the beginning of a long nightmare.

I ended up having two part time jobs because my retail job was only part time and a full time position was not available. So I was working part time at two different retail stores. I would leave my sons with my mom when I worked. My mom was a day care provider for other kids.

I hated that my sons and I were living at my mom's. I was grateful for the roof over my head and for her babysitting while I worked but, my mom was getting very angry with me. The longer I stayed there I knew the worse it would get. My mother never talked about her feelings, she yelled about her feelings! She would tell me what a loser I was, how I had messed up again. She would yell that she wouldn't keep watching the boys forever. She called me terrible names and we argued constantly. More than anything I wanted my own place. I wanted to have a place of my own where my boys and I could live but, I just didn't make enough money. I had to get a car and I had a car payment. My mom did cosign for the car so I could get it. I made every payment; I was never late on that payment, not once. My mom threw the car up in my face on a regular basis. Without her I wouldn't have a car, without her I wouldn't have a roof over my head, without her I wouldn't have a babysitter for the boys while I worked. I probably told her thank you a million times. I tried and tried my best while living there. I just couldn't please her. I truly was thankful to her and yet I would cry in my bed at night. I didn't want the boys subjected to her verbal abuse. I wanted a peaceful loving environment for them.

One day Lily called me at work. Jack had fallen on the basement steps and his lip was bleeding. I was now asst. manager at the retail store and working full time. Mom was screaming that she couldn't be responsible for the boys it was too much on her. She screamed that I was ungrateful, a terrible mother and on and on. When I got to her house, she was on one of her verbal rampages. She was screaming at me, she was screaming at the boys, I was crying and the boys were crying. I got the boys and we left the house. I put the boys in the back seat of my car. I screamed at the boys, "You two have got to be good or grandma is going to kick us out. If she kicks us out you both will be in an orphanage!"

Mike Rogers

LOVING ME

The minute I screamed I saw the look on Abe's face. Such a dear little boy, both of them were fantastic kids. I had hurt both of them with my words. I had never screamed at them like that before. I had never said hurtful things to them before. I told them I was sorry and I told them I would take them to their dad's (Abe called Gus dad). I was sobbing. I pulled in front of Gus's (he was living in the house we had bought while we were married, without a care). I got the boys out of the back seat and we went up to his door. I knocked on the door and Gus answered.

I explained to him that the boys couldn't stay at my mom's anymore. Mom had said that it was just too much for her. I ask him if he would please let the boys live there with him until I could afford a small apartment. I was crying so hard I could barely talk. I asked him, I begged him to please just help me with the boys. Please let me share parenting with him, please let me pick them up when I wasn't working, please just work with me on taking care of the boys together. Gus said he would. He agreed to us being civil over the sharing of custody of the boys. I kissed the boys good bye, and Gus took them inside and slammed the door in my face. He wouldn't let me in the house. I was crying so hard I could barely make it to my car. I tried to drive but had to pull over; I opened my car door and vomited. I laid my body down in the front seat of my car, sobbing on the side of a road and cried and cried. It got dark outside and I slept in my car. I was too mad and too hurt to try and go back to my mom's house.

REFLECTION

There is the saying that hindsight is 20/20. I think about this now and there are so many things I wish I had done differently. But this was the straw that broke the camel's back and led me to LifeWay, to the start of healing, to a deeper relationship with Jesus and to my friendship with Ann. I am thankful for all of that.

1991 Dr. Hanson

I CAN'T BEGIN to describe the anguish that I felt. I hated myself. Shame, fear, anger and hurt were just some of the destructive emotions that took possession of my soul. I wanted to die, in fact I made a plan to overdose on some medications my doctor has prescribed. I longed for an end to all my pain and all the hopelessness. The only hope I had was the love I had for my two sons. That love penetrated all other darkness. I struggled with my roller coaster of emotions. I could die and not feel the pain anymore or I could live and try to help myself and my sons. I had reached the point where I knew I couldn't choose life and succeed by myself. Even my church left me; I felt they were siding with Gus. I felt I had no support and I had lost everything of value to me and had no friends or family to which I could turn. I prayed and I simply told God that if He wanted me to live and if there was any purpose in my life then He would have to step in and carry me. I had reached the end. I was one step away from death.

My general physician was a wonderful Christian lady and by God's favor she would save my life. Her name was Dr. Pamela Hanson. I drove myself to her office. I walked in and when the receptionist asked if she could help me, I simply answer. "Yes, I am a patient of Dr. Hanson and I need to see her now or I will surely die." I was crying so hard I could barely speak.

She took me straight back to a patient room. I looked like hell. I had slept in my clothes. I was a mess. I couldn't stop crying. I was 30 years old and I weigh 98 pounds.

When Dr. Hanson came into the room she took one look at me and rushed to my side. She embraced me. She asked me when was the last time that I had eaten. I couldn't remember. I couldn't stop crying, I was trying to tell her everything. It just started pouring out of me. I was crying so hard that I almost started to hyperventilate.
She had a nurse bring me crackers from her lunch that she had packed that day and a soft drink. Dr. Hanson told me to try and take some bites, to try and drink. She listened as I cried on and on and was trying to tell her what a failure I was and all that happen and how Gus had the boys and I just wanted to die.

It was November 1991 and God sent me not one lifeline but many that day. Dr. Hanson told me about LifeWay. LifeWay was located in Emerson North Hospital. I could sign myself in for severe depression and receive the help I longed for. Dr. Hanson was gentle and kind; she talked to me softly and told me there was hope. In her office that day she was more than my doctor, she was a lifeline, a friend.

1991 LifeWay

A SHORT TIME later I walked in LifeWay. A nurse met me at the door. She took my hand. Dr. Hanson had called ahead and I am sure she told them just how bad a shape I was in for this nurse was as gentle and kind as an angel. Maybe she was an angel. She helped me fill out paperwork. She took me to my room. I had nothing but the clothes on my back. I was given a private room with a private bathroom. Food was sent to my room and I tried to eat. I answered a lot of questions and I was so very tired. I took a hot shower and was given a hospital gown to sleep in because I had nothing with me.

> *The words of the reckless pierce like swords, but the tongue of the wise brings healing.*
> Proverbs 12:18

Founded only two years earlier, LifeWay integrated medicine, psychotherapy, family interactions, prayer, Bible studies, and group dynamics in a residential as well as outpatient format. It talked of being a Christian community and using faith along with medicine and psychology which made me scared at first. I would come to realize that this Christian community treated not my symptoms but me. It was not my sickness but my "wholeness" – my body, mind, and soul - that was to grow. It was here that I first learned that I was a victim and what had happened to me was not my fault. It was here that I began to lose my stinking thinking; it was here I began to change.

Be transformed by the renewing of your mind.
Romans 12:2

Going into LifeWay was difficult. The class, the therapy, all of it, was difficult, painful and emotionally draining. But it was also healing. At the time I was uncomfortable with it being Christian. Although I had gotten saved at age 12 while going to church with my friend Paula, I never felt holy. I never felt good enough. I have carried this spirit of shame, this stinking thinking, all of my life. Many times it has come close to destroying me. Today I still work at destroying it!

Ever since I was saved, I never doubted that Jesus was the son of God and that he died on the cross for me. I never doubted his love. I didn't always feel it, but I knew His love was real and unconditional. I read my Bible regularly. I prayed, oh did I pray! I would go to Bible studies and church. I didn't let anyone get too close to me at churches or these groups because deep inside I was always carrying this heavy weight of shame. I wasn't a holy Christian lady; I was a bad person who had lied, gotten pregnant out of wedlock, etc. The messages I received on how to live a Godly life from church members who looked like they had it all together only brought me more shame. Still I never doubted that God loved me so I just moved on - church to church. I didn't feel like I would ever be holy enough to fit in with the other holy ladies. I just didn't realize at the time that I had been abused and that because of the messages I had received and believed this spirit of shame was a stronghold that was out to destroy me. But God had other plans!

When someone is a victim of sexual abuse, verbal abuse, financial abuse, physical abuse, any abuse there are messages that they receive that they take in to their soul and they take root there and grow and fester. Shame is one of the biggest ones. I felt shameful when my father molested me. I felt shameful when Gary, a teenage boy, in our neighborhood played games with me that was sexual and I was only 10 and 11 at the time. I felt shame when Ted insisted that if I loved him, what he wanted to do to me was right. I felt shame when I lied. Mixed with that shame were feelings that I wanted to make my dad happy. I wanted to be liked by Gary and receive attention. I wanted Ted to love me. I wanted to be loved. I had been taught that it was okay to lie to protect someone you care about. My father taught me to lie about the abuse. My mother taught me to lie about dad's violence, about Oscar her lover, and about her verbal and sometimes physical abuse. Ted taught me to lie and the lying never stopped.

Along with all this abuse I had received mixed messages….. The messages that I, as a child, received were confusing and conflicting. After the statutory rape my mom called me terrible names. I was a liar because I hadn't told her the truth about what was going on. I couldn't be trusted! I was a whore! Over sexed! A filthy whore who could never be a Christian!! She said these things to her broken and abused daughter. It wasn't about trust, a 13 year old girl needs parenting and guidance and protection. My mother never talked to me about sex. She never talked to me about love and relationships. I doubt if she knew herself what God's intention was for man and woman. She allowed a man to move in and live and court and groom her 13 year old daughter. It is not a parent's job to be their child's friend; it is their job to love, nurture and protect their child. You cannot trust children to make adult choices.

REFLECTION

As Sandy, my counselor, recently pointed out, current research into the teenage brain makes clear that the human brain isn't fully developed until people are well into their twenties. Previously it was thought that the teenage brain was just "an adult brain with fewer miles on it." It turns out that the frontal lobes, which are associated with choosing and decision making as well as with impulse control and emotional management, are not fully connected- they lack the myelin coating that allows efficient communication between sections of the brain. And here I was at 30 years of age totally unable to help myself.

John & I met with Dr. Sweeten in July of 2015 to talk about my time at LifeWay. Based on my life story he was amazed I had survived!

1991 Lifeway Journals

I HAVE ALL my journals from 1991 on. As I read this I cry. I can't describe how painful all of this was and still is when I think about it. Even though it was so painful emotionally for me at the time LifeWay was hope – hope for a better tomorrow. As long as a person has hope they can face just about anything. I hope this book gives someone hope for a better tomorrow.

My journal's notes from my first day at LifeWay…

November 6, 1991 Wednesday 6:00 pm

I'm at Emerson North hospital scared to death! I'm about to be admitted to LifeWay - maybe they can help me. Maybe God is finally helping me. I'm scared, real scared. I have a feeling that I am in for a bumpy ride. God be with me. I'll be here for at least two weeks. I know I won't have a job, but maybe I'll have a life. God I worry about everything. I worry about my kids. Lord write the way across the sky. I haven't told my mom I am here yet. She is going to shit!

November 6, 1991 Wednesday 10:00 pm

I'm in my room at Emerson North Hospital. I think treatment here will be good for me. Oh, God I pray so. It's a Christian organization. Don't know how I feel about that. I'm scared about what is going to take place here. I pray for healing. I'm lonely and scared. I called Gus, he said Abe is sick. I wish I could be with him. I wish I was well enough to care for him. I love him and Bear (my name for Jack) so very much. I can't face tomorrow without them. Tomorrow is the first day of the rest of my life. I'm so scared.

November 7, 1991 Thursday 10:00 am
I've been up since 6:30 am. It's a busy schedule here. So far I've talked to Dr. Newton my psychiatrist and had a "Rational Christian Thinking" class, a TB test and an EKG test. I'm tired and would like to take a nap because I didn't sleep well last night. The people in my group are very, very kind. I feel awkward and shy. I pray Abe is doing well.

REFLECTION

All I could think about was my boys. I had to heal. I had to get well so I could give them a better life. I didn't care about myself at the time. I didn't think I mattered. I didn't like myself at all. I thought I was a bad person.

November 7, 1991 Thursday 5:30 pm
Today has been so busy: one thing after another, one class after another. LifeWay runs a tight schedule. I have to get away from my mom. She is so destructive. Always has a mean thing to say!

November 7, 1991 Thursday 8:40 pm
I talked to Abe on the phone. I asked him to forgive me. He is such a dear, dear boy. I pray for healing. I am looking forward to healing. There is a very kind nurse here, her name is Lenora. She loaned me a book called The Prophet by Kahlil Gibran. It is beautiful.

REFLECTION

Asking a 9 year old boy to forgive me for not being there for him, how scared and confused he must have been. I don't know what he was hearing about me. There was no way for him to know at the time that by getting help, I was making the future better for him and Jack because then I could be the mother they deserved.

November 8, 1991 Friday 12:55 pm

I am tired. I just finished lunch and the days here are difficult. We did an exercise in "Ropes" class. We all got in a circle and all our hands were tied together - we had to get loose without removing the ropes from around our wrists. We wiggled every way we could. We just seemed to get in more of a mess. Just like life - you struggle and try and try and you only end up more in a mess. What is the answer? Why? I'm sad and lonely. No family, no friends!

REFLECTION

The years of abuse had taught me that I was powerless, guilty, and shameful; in short my life was a mess. At LifeWay I was learning not to get into the mess in the first place.

November 8, 1991 Friday 4:30pm

I just talked to mom on the phone. I wanted her to bring my contact solution tomorrow, if she visits. She said, "She didn't know if she could visit because Sissy had to work at Sam's. I asked, if Joe my brother could bring her. Mom answered, "I don't know. They all think you're faking it. (Faking it?!?! I scream to myself.) How can someone fake such pain? How can someone hurt so deep and others not see the pain? I hate my family. I hate them. I hate my mom, I hate my brothers. I hate my sister. I hate Ted, I hate Gus, I hate! And I am sad and I hurt! I will try to hang on and I will try one second at a time to survive.

REFLECTION

So much hurt and pain was inside me at the time. I was broken! I see now how in many ways we were all badly wounded. I was trying to heal but they were so wounded themselves they could not see it. This one is hard to share. I didn't really hate my mom or my family, my brothers. I was angry at them and angry at some of the ways they had treated me. I was hurt and scared. Emotions were pouring out. Sometimes I feel going through these journals, writing this book is like pouring alcohol on an open wound. I have tried to stuff, hide all the ugliness for so long. But the only way to really be free and to help myself and others is to let the alcohol rinse the wounds, washing all the pain out.

In order to heal, I first needed to identify the beliefs that I created to protect me from the trauma of my life, the unhealthy beliefs that were destructive to my wellbeing. I had to stop blaming myself and place the blame on the perpetrators. I had to stop pleasing others and begin to respect myself. I came to realize that I needed boundaries and that I had rights which others needed to honor.

November 9, 1991 *Saturday 7:15 pm* "Loving Me"
> *Today I wrote a poem about and to my mom, but, I am not sure if I will give it to her. It's a way for me to speak and come to an agreement that my mother will probably never change, but I have. I have learned how to set boundaries and how to no longer give her words permission to destroy me anymore.*

After a couple days at LifeWay I was asked if I could leave my private room and share a room with another female patient because a male patient was being admitted and they needed the room for him. They talked about health and happiness growing out of developing fulfilling relationships and that I had been alone too long and needed to work on my interpersonal relationship skills.

I dreaded leaving my private room. It was a sanctuary, a safe haven but I did agree to move. This was a God thing. What I mean by God thing is that all along my life God has placed people, events, and blessings in my life at just the very moment I needed them the most. I didn't know it then but moving into that room with another female patient was going to be one of the greatest gifts God has ever given me.

When I moved into the room my new roommate was a senior citizen. She was old enough to be my mother. In fact Ann was just a couple years younger than my mom. She was in LifeWay because she had been married for 30 something years and it was an abusive relationship. She had finally gotten the courage to leave the marriage and she was suffering from depression caused by all that was going on in her life. She was an amazing Christian lady and people who didn't accept that she had left her husband and family were unsupportive. I won't write anymore on how she was feeling and struggling because that is not my story to tell. At first I was not thrilled at having a roommate and certainly not a senior citizen. Mother figures didn't appeal to me at the time. Ann was dreading a roommate too and when she saw that I was young she dreaded it more. She wanted peace and quiet and feared that because I was young I would have a ton of visitors every night. Boy, was she wrong!

Soon Ann and I started talking in the evening in the quiet of our room. We had classes together and were learning the reasons behind our depression, but in those evening hours we talked and started to bond. She was an amazing woman: kind, loving, gentle, quiet, Christian, proper, from an affluent family and well raised. Not what you usually picture when you think of abusive relationships.

We both were in deep emotional pain and felt like we could trust no one and that we wore a scarlet letter to all the Christians out there. We had something else in common too. We both had deep faith! Unbreakable, unmovable faith! Not faith in people, or churches, or religion but certainly in God, in His son and the relationship and love we knew we had from Him. Unfortunately the church shoots its own broken sometimes. People are easily capable of getting on their high horse, pointing, judging and condemning, when I feel we as a church should be more open, forgiving, healing and loving.

My time was short at LifeWay - nine days -because my insurance wouldn't pay for it. But I came out of there with HOPE. For the first time in my life I had hope that my life was not only going to be different but much, much better.

They taught me boundaries and self-worth, they gave me unconditional love. Nothing I confessed to them shocked them and nothing I said brought pointing fingers or judgment. They wanted to equip me with skills to live a better live and to be independent. They told me everything I needed for change was already inside ME! I believed. I could see a pathway to change. They did not just treat my symptoms but the whole me. Treating symptoms doesn't cure a person but unfortunately medicine today is all about symptom treatment because that is how doctors, hospitals, clinicians are paid. Manage Care pays by the symptom – identify a symptom, write a prescription that will manage it and the insurance will pay. Manage Care also demands this be done in a short and quick period of time per visit. LifeWay went beyond that. They took time to engage me; they took the time to make me feel I was a person to be respected. They took the time to go beyond my symptoms and helped me regain control of my life.

Up until now I had run from relationship to relationship, looking for someone to love me, rescue me. I was looking for my prince charming riding in on a white horse and to take me away from all the pain. LifeWay was worried that I would fall into the same old trap of marrying a man to rescue me. They stressed that I needed to establish myself on my own two feet without relying on someone else heavily. They saw two positives which they built on. The first was that I did graduate from high school even though that final year I was married to an alcoholic and drug user who did not want me to finish school. The second was that I had been working since March and doing well in my job. The staff at LifeWay had been so supportive in those nine days that I was beginning to think I might be able to carry on. One thing for sure I dropped my stinking thinking of suicide. I hadn't given it much thought that my prince has already loved me, rescued me and died for me. Jesus was all I needed:

> *I can do all things through Christ which strengthens me.*
> Philippians 4:13

After I left LifeWay's Residential Program I continued with their outpatient therapy to help me heal. I took a boundaries class, a damaged emotion class, Bible studies, therapy, everything that spoke life and healing; I grabbed it and drank it in.

After Ann got out we would go to groups and studies together. We loved each other. She knew everything about me, everything and she cherished me. I knew everything about her, everything and I cherished her. I didn't realize it at the time but, she became a mother figure to me. We went to movies together, plays and lunches. We encouraged each other in our dark times and when we felt shame we reminded each other that Jesus loved us and we kept each other going.

Gus had a girlfriend now. She was a much younger girlfriend. Together they had decided that they could just shut me out of the boys' lives. I was about to face one of my fiercest storms and as I look back now, I see how God kept me from drowning.

Laura Kagawa-Burke

REFLECTION

Fighting Gus over the boys was one of the worst times of my life! Yes, I know that considering what I have been through that is saying a lot. But what he put me through, trying to keep me from seeing the boys felt like getting stabbed again and again. The blocked phone, not being there when I was supposed to pick the boys up, the arguments didn't have to be that way. I will be forever sorry that my sons had to go through that.

In fighting Gus I was establishing my boundaries, I wasn't there to please him I was there to protect my boys and it gave me a sense of self-worth. Each time I cast off an old belief I gained some space to be myself or at least to realize there was a person inside me that needed to be allowed to live. It might have seemed to be a new person but in reality it was an old person. It was the person I was created to be finally seeing the light of day.

1991 Trish

AFTER LIFEWAY I moved in with Trish, my friend from work. She and a friend shared an apartment and they had a small spare bedroom with a twin bed in it. She offered it to me free of charge. I could live there, work and attend out-patient therapy. I could learn and grow and become independent. It was an answered prayer. Here I was at the lowest, most desperate point in my life and I had no place to go. My insurance ran out for LifeWay and when the staff tried to find a Halfway House for me they were told I was not sick enough! My mood was of extreme sadness for the failures and the mess I had made. At times I thought of suicide as the way to end this nightmare, I often cried so much my speech was difficult to understand. I was so agitated that my thoughts were disconnected; judgment and insights were poor or lacking. How much farther could I deteriorate to qualify for the Halfway House!

When the boys came to Trish's to visit I would lay pallets of covers on the floor beside my twin bed and they would sleep there. As long as they were with me and I was there, I had peace.

Gus and Tami (his girlfriend) blocked their phone from receiving my calls. I would try to call and it would say the phone was blocked. I would go to a phone booth to call from a number they were not familiar with and Tami or Gus would answer. They would always tell me the boys couldn't come to the phone.

I would schedule a time to pick them up and arrive at their house to find them gone, no one home. Although this was very stressful and I cried a million tears I did not give up! LifeWay had helped me gain some independence and belief in myself. I was stronger and mad! I became a room mother and volunteered at every school event there was so I could see the boys. I would go in to work in the mornings, arrange my schedule for a lunch or two hours off run to school, run back to work, and work until closing. I would find out if there was a sport event, a parent teacher conference, a classroom party as far as possible ahead of time and I would either plan my day off on that event day or work a half shift go to the event and then back to work to close the store. It was hard and I was exhausted, but there was no way Gus was keeping me from my kids.

I knew Gus was mad at me, really mad, I had left, I was growing as a person, I was an assistant manager now, I had my own car and I was living at Trish's apartment in peace. I had still managed to communicate with the boys and I even ate lunch with them at school. He wasn't defeating me and he was mad!

I thought long and hard and prayed on how I should continue writing about this part of my life. There is a hurt person inside of me that wants to write down every mean, selfish thing that Gus and Tami did to keep me from the boys, but if I accept Jesus' forgiveness for my sins and if I am to love and forgive like He does than I must for my own wellbeing and for the sakes of my sons, simply write only what is needed and forgive them.

I was not without my own faults as you can clearly read in my story. I had jumped from relationship to relationship and I was very dependent until I went into LifeWay. I understand now why I made the decisions I made, but that still doesn't make them right. So I will say this. When two adults get divorced and children are involved, it is devastating to the children. Even in the best of divorces where both adults can be adult like and mature, children still have a lot of feelings and emotions to work through. When two grown adults fight over custody and use the kids as a tool trying to get back at another it is the child that hurts. You are abusing the innocent child that loves both parents and that doesn't want to betray either parent by choosing sides. Children are not capable of choosing sides. Nor should they ever have to. So if divorce is inevitable and must happen then please as much as you think you now hate the person you were once married to, please be mature enough and civil enough to give and share, and allow both parents to be in the child's life as much as possible. That is as long as each parent is not abusive or harmful to the child.

The more Gus dished out the more I fought. One day I hadn't been able to get a hold of Jack. He had missed school because he was sick. Gus or Tami would not allow me to speak to Jack on the phone or tell me how sick he was. I showed up at their door. I was in the doorway and Tami and I were having a confrontation. I wanted to know what was wrong with Jack. Whenever Jack got sick it was usually with his throat and he would usually end up with strep throat. I wanted to take him to the doctor. (I paid for all the doctor visits, their clothes, etc.) Tami told me that she was Jack's mom now and that she could care for him. She pushed me, trying to get me back outside the door and I slapped her. I had never slapped a person before. But when she said that she was Jack's mom now.......I reacted in a very immature manner. Gus immediately got in between us. He was as surprised as I was that I had reacted physically. It was wrong of me to do, but I was their mom and I reached my breaking point because I ended up taking Jack to the doctor. He did have strep throat and needed an antibiotic. I went back to Gus's took Jack up to his room (the house was still in both of our names) and sat on the floor next to him until he fell asleep. I cried a lot that night. I look back and blame myself a lot for not taking the boys to Trish's and keeping them. But I had no one to watch them while I worked and I was still weak in a lot of areas. I can't go back and undo the past. No one can, but I gave it my all at the time. Maybe my all wasn't good enough, I don't know, but there wasn't a moment that those boys didn't know that I loved them. Gus would tell them horrible things about me. I never said a bad word about Gus while they were little. Oh they knew we fought and they knew I had to continue to fight for every minute to see them, but I didn't degrade Gus to them. And I tried to be civil and talk instead of yell and I tried to explain to Gus that he was hurting the boys in all the fighting. Every minute that I had with them they had all of my attention. My life was the boys, work, and therapy. It stayed that way for quite a while.

REFLECTION

I had made so many bad choices. I chose wrong types, bad relationships. All the times I didn't know how to make better choices. But something good came out of my pain. Pain taught me to choose wisely. Pain teaches us to choose differently.

Much is written about pain and suffering, some folks allow their lives to be identified by their suffering. They use their suffering as a crutch and continue to exist in their suffering while all the time letting others folks carry them. Sometimes they do so because they are afraid of making changes. They are afraid of the unknown; but, it is only in intentionally making the changes that we grow. It reminds me of a story I read about the trapeze. We can stay holding tight to one bar and continue to swing high above the ground. But in making the exchange of bars, in moving to the other, in that seemingly scary suspended moment of reaching out, letting go and grabbing the new bar do we grow. We recognize a danger, work through it and grow in skills, ability, and confidence. So it is with suffering. We can allow it to drive us away from our true self and even away from our God and His all-encompassing love. We can allow it to block our understanding that

God is our source of protection and refuge. Or we can embrace Him, partner with Him, and ask Him to help us make the life-enriching changes. It is a choice we make and a choice we make intentionally, not by chance. The only change with meaning is the change made intentionally.

1991 Ann

―――― ~⚬~ ――――

Forgiveness is letting go of thought, belief, and need that
the past could have been and should have been different.
Oprah Winfrey

AFTER A WHILE Trish had to move back to her home town and I was
once again without a place to live. I moved back into my mom's, I had
asked her if I could please move back for a while and she said yes. After
I got moved in to my room at my mom's I asked her to sit down so I
could talk to her. I could tell that she didn't like the idea of me asking
her to sit down. But I said "Please just give me a minute."

I sat across from her at the dining room table and I reached over and
took her hand. She was surprised I could tell, but she didn't jerk her
hand away. I looked her straight in the eyes and said, "Mom I know I
have hurt you and I know I have disappointed you. I am sorry. I hope
you can please forgive me for every hurt I have caused you." You could
have heard a pin drop!
She was not expecting that from me. I was very sincere. She mumbled
something in return, like thank you for saying that. I got up, hugged
her and went to my room.

And another amazing thing happened to me. A few weeks before I
moved back into mom's house, I was in a support group with my friend

Ann. We went to a lot of different groups together. I was sharing about my teenage pregnancy and the trauma and pain I experience. I shared how my mom and I had never talked, never mentioned what had happened. I was crying and hurting.

Ann got out of her chair and knelt in front of me and the entire group. She took my hand. I didn't know what she was doing. "Vicki," she said, "I am your mom and I love you. I am so sorry that I didn't protect you. I am so sorry that I allowed you to go in harm's way. I am sorry that I didn't cherish you as my daughter. I am so sorry this happened to you and that you went through this terrible trauma. I am to blame. Will you please forgive me?'

Ann was role playing. She was stepping in for my mother, saying what I had always longed to hear from my mom and what my mom couldn't say to me.

Everyone in the group was crying. I hugged Ann so tight and I sobbed and sobbed. What she had just done for me was the most beautiful thing that anyone had ever done for me. She gave me a beautiful gift. She set me free.

I can't explain how or why that meant so much, only that it was the most beautiful gift of love that anyone had given me. I knew right away I could forgive my mom and even my dad. I would never hear from them that they had ever done anything wrong. For whatever reason they couldn't give me that. So I had carried the weight of the blame. For some reason after Ann said that I knew the truth. I knew that I had been a young girl and that I hadn't been protected or cherished. I also knew that I didn't want to carry around the weight of resentment or bitterness anymore and I didn't want to hate my parents. I would never give them the power over me to hate, or to turn me into a bitter person. They had had enough power over me; now it was gone. And I certainly wanted to apologize to those I had hurt. I never wanted them to carry any weight of bitterness or hate that I may have caused.

So I went to work and spent time with the boys and when they spent the night, I was always with them. My mom was never alone with them. I refused to argue with her. There were times when we would be in the car together, maybe I was running her on an errand or something and she would start with her down grading or abusive talk. I would simply pull over my car and look right at her and say, "Mom if you are going to talk like that, then I will have to take you back home" or "Mom, you can't talk like that in front of the boys." Sometimes she would start yelling to me "This is my house" or "I will kick you out." But I would just say fine kick me out and I would leave the room. Sometimes I had to calmly leave the house and drive for long periods of time until I knew she had calmed down. Sometimes I went in my room and locked the door and put on head phones while she ranted. It really does take two people to argue. It was not easy. I hated it. I hated living there but, I was stronger and I was learning and growing and I think she saw that.

REFLECTION

When I think of Ann I am reminded of this Bible verse:

> *If one falls down His friend can help him up.*
> *But pity the man who falls and has no one to help him.*
> Ecclesiastes 4:10

God sent so many friends into my life, each of them giving me a hand, helping me up! As you read this book you will see evidence of God's great love for me. My friend Jesus and all those along my life journey reaching out, offering hope and love. Most of all they, like Ann, taught and showed me that I was not powerless. I had power to control my life to let myself grow going forward. Maybe I was powerless when I was abused but I am not powerless now. I have the power to move past the abuse, to move past the impact these traumas have had on my life and to rediscover and restore the internal abilities that make me the person God created me to be. It has taken work, hard-hard work and the support of loving, open and non-judgmental friends. People who from the very beginning have been empathic, who have accepted me as I was, and let me talk without judging me. It is hard work to dig deep to expose my unhealthy belief systems and the internal walls that I built to protect myself from the traumas. Then and only then can I understand them and begin to break hem down and clean them out.

1991 Count

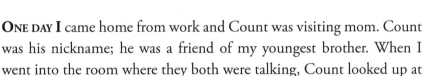

ONE DAY I came home from work and Count was visiting mom. Count was his nickname; he was a friend of my youngest brother. When I went into the room where they both were talking, Count looked up at me. "Hey Vicki," he said, "I was wondering how many times have you been saved?"

Mom sat there with a smirk on her face. I knew she had put him up to it. She was trying to get a reaction out of me and she was always telling me how I was not nor could I ever be a Christian. I turned around and went upstairs to my room. Once again I locked the door and cried. Looking back at it now, what I wish I had done was this.

I wish I had stood there tall and proud, I wish I had looked him in the eyes and said, "Once Count when I was 12 years old I heard the wonderful news that Jesus loved me, that he loved me enough to die for me and that he loves me unconditionally. It is a pure and forever kind of love, a never ending kind of love. I have never had anyone love me unconditionally before and I wish that I would have been nurtured more in my walk with Jesus. I wish I had done better, made better choices. But I'm growing Count, I'm learning and I will be a better person. So the answer would be once Count, once and it was the beginning of my being."

I can't go back to yesterday because I was a different person then. Lewis Carroll

I didn't say that because at the time I was hurt and still not quite strong enough. I look back now and wonder why a mother would allow a person to say something like that to their child, why a mother would put someone up to saying that. Because of words like that it would take years before I could truly forgive myself for all the relationships I had gotten in, for all the pain I had caused. It would be years before I could sit in a church and feel like I was just as lovable as the Christian lady who had grown up in a loving Christian home. Because of the words that had been spoken to me, over me, I carried shame for many, many years. I still have to work on not carrying it today. Because of those kinds of ugly words I always compared my mistakes to others and I always felt like my mistakes or sins were far worse. Even though Jesus loved me, I would never be the Christian church lady that I so wanted to be.

My mom, my family, sometimes even church people had placed the scarlet letter on me and it took a long time for me to realize that the blood of Jesus had already taken all of that to the cross. Today as I write this I am still guarded even around my church family. I still have moments when I think I am not good enough or holy enough or like other church ladies. I have to remind myself that it is the enemy telling me lies.

Was I living a Christian life at the time? This is the only answer I can give you. I had unshakable faith. I prayed, I read my Bible not because it was a rule of church people but because I loved talking with God. I loved Him. I read my Bible because I wanted to get to know Him, to hear of His great love. I have read my Bible through several times. Not because it is a Christian rule but because I delight in my relationship with Jesus. I learn new things about my Savior every time I read it. I worship my Savior not because it is expected of me but because I have this amazing love relationship with Him and I want to worship Him. I go to church not because my pastor or a Christian friend says I should. I go because it is there that I sing to Him and learn about his compassion and grace and meet more people to love.

As a matter of fact I have never let anyone bully me into doing what they think a Christian should do. If I am doing it for them or because they say so, then I am doing it for the wrong reasons. And I won't let someone bully me into believing that because of my mistakes I can't be a strong, beautiful Christian lady. I am one, God says so!

REFLECTION

Of course I still struggle with some self-degradation. The good thing is now I can catch myself if I am doing negative self-talk or believing negatively about myself. I catch myself and try to turn it around. I try to apply what I have learned, the truth that God loves me and thinks I am awesome! Sometimes I fall into the pit of despair and I really struggle to get my thoughts back on God's Truth. But I know I have the power to control how I respond to others, to their words, to their actions. I know myself and have enough self-awareness to know when I am becoming disconnected from the Truth and am not being my true self. I know there is more to me than what others say about or do to me. I continue to hold onto the joy of knowing God loves me.

1992 Jim

MY DIVORCE FROM Gus was finally finalized. Abe would live with me and Jack with Gus, but on Wednesdays I would have Jack and Abe overnight and every other weekend the boys would be at my house together. Jack would be there during spring break, summer vacation with Gus and me taking turns on holidays.

After I had gotten a lawyer and a parenting specialist was appointed over our case, Gus had to listen to the courts recommendation. No more blocked phone calls, or not allowing me to see the boys. It had been a horrible battle and Abe and Jack had suffered the most through it all.

I have told the boys I am sorry for all the pain. I never meant to hurt them but Gus and I both did. Through love and forgiveness the boys have grown into amazing young men who love the Lord and have great faith. We have a good relationship where we can talk about anything (and we have) and we are always telling each other how much we love each other. Abe is married to a wonderful Christian lady named Amy. She is my daughter through marriage. We too have a good relationship and I thank God for all of them.

In March of 1992 I was working full time as assistant manager at Chess King, a man's clothing store. One day this very nice looking man came into the store. He was going on vacation to Florida with some of the firefighters he worked with and needed some clothes. We talked easily to each other. I helped him pick out a few outfits and he tried them on. He stayed at the store for a while, talking, trying on clothes, shopping and we were talking and laughing about clothes. When he was ready to check out he wrote a check. Back then a lot of people had their phone number on their checks. By the time he was ready for check out, we had been doing a little flirting with each other. He handed me the check and I saw his phone number on it. I told him that I was going to call and talk dirty to him sometime. (Joking) He laughed.

When he left I knew I would see him again. I just knew it. I felt better about myself than I ever had. I was still taking classes and talking to my counselor. Later on that day when I was closing the shop and closing out the cash drawer, I saw Jim's check there with his phone number on it. I smiled and wrote down his phone number. When I called that number and asked for Jim some guy answered the phone and I assumed it was his roommate. The guy told me that Jim was sleeping and asked if he could take a message so I tried to think of something to say. Suddenly I blurred out, "Tell him Vicki called and was going to talk dirty to him, but he missed it." Then I left my phone number and hung up.

I started laughing when I got off the phone. I couldn't believe I had just done that, but it was fun. Jim called me back once he got the message and laughed at the message I had left. We have been married almost 23 years and I still haven't talked dirty to him, but I tease him that someday I just might!

The funny thing about the message is that the guy who answered my call wasn't Jim's roommate, he was Jim's brother! (Jim had been in a bad relationship before and had moved back home after the break up.) Jim's brother had written down my message about calling to talk dirty to him and left it on the kitchen table. Jim's parents saw the note on their kitchen table that said, "Jim, Vicki called to talk dirty to you and you missed it. Here is her number."

Oh my goodness! When Jim told me that his parents had seen the message, I about died! The first time I met them, I was so embarrassed. I kept telling them that I wasn't really going to talk dirty to him.

When Jim and I started dating, I wasn't looking for a husband or a relationship. In fact I had grown enough to realize that I just wanted to continue to grow as a person and take care of my sons. I told Jim from the start that I had been hurt and didn't want to get serious. He told me about himself being hurt and that he had the same walls up. But, we kept dating.

Jim was different than any other guy I had ever dated or been with. He was a hard worker-- stable, responsible, kind, and gentle. He came from a good respectable family. His parents had married and stayed together until death. He had aunts, uncles, cousins, grandparents, family events and love. He had grown up in a safe warm, loving environment.

After a few dates I told Jim everything! I felt comfortable in talking with him and I felt like I had known him forever. I didn't know what he would think about me, being married before, my bad relationships, the teen pregnancy, everything, but I told him. I saw Jim again and again after telling him everything. He didn't run away. He didn't judge me or think less of me. We fell in love with each other.

Six months after we met, in September of 1992 we married, in spite of ourselves. It was fast and the odds were against us, just look at my record. But there were a lot of things different. I was different. I had fallen into a pit of despair and hurt before and had climbed my way out into healing and love. I had a good support system of loyal friends and groups and therapy. I had fought Gus over the boys and I had fought my way into the more peaceful relationship with my mom. The relationship with my mom would never be as good as I would want, but it was better. God had made a commitment to love me when He died on the cross and now Jim and I were making a commitment to each other.

REFLECTION

I have learned that as I grow and change my belief systems there will be those around me who cannot grow, who will not be able to meet the "new" me. In making that acknowledgement I have shown the depth of my growth in self-power, self-awareness and being my authentic self.

I can now identify dysfunction. I know it when I see it. I can set boundaries better than I ever had before. I don't need a man. I don't need to be rescued. I have God as the love of my life and as my strength and guidance. This time I see things differently. My head is together better than it has ever been before. I am continuing to get help and support. I know I still need to grow and heal and I am working on my mental health really hard. I know now that love is not only a feeling but, a commitment.

1992 Gus

Journal Entry - 9/7/92 Monday 9:50 pm

After work I went to Gus's to pick up Abe. He was supposed to be there at 6:00 but, never got home until 8:30pm. Abe said they had some car trouble. I saw Jack. He started to cry. I held him and talked to him, my heart was breaking. I ask Gus if I could take Jack for an ice cream after school tomorrow - he said no!

Gus said that he wouldn't be going to work until late. I don't know what that has to do with it. Gus just loves being in control! I love you Jack, someday we all will be together.

Journal Entry - 9/9/92 Wednesday 8:00 pm

I feel very drained! I'm emotionally exhausted! Gus wouldn't let me have Jack yesterday or today. He is being a butt! I called my lawyer but, no money, no help! Life sucks!

THERE IS A part of me sometimes that gets angry at you God and it wouldn't do any good to lie about it. You know. Especially when it comes to the part in my life when I struggled so and fought so hard for a better life for Abe and Jack. I was so tired God, I was so weary. I didn't have any resources; if I did I couldn't find them.

How many times did I cry for those boys and how many times did those boys cry for me? How many times did I crawl my way out of bed, go to work, go to therapy and argue with Gus and fight to spend time with them? How many times did I make myself keep going and force myself not to give up and go on? How many days in court and lawyers and fighting and how many times did I succeed or fail? With each success I felt like I had taken a giant leap and with each failure I felt like I couldn't take one more step.

I remember one time when I had had enough! Enough of all the fighting! Enough of all the games Gus played. He would block my phone so I couldn't call the boys when they were with him. He would say I could pick up the boys and I would go there to get them and they would be gone. He would fight and scream and argue. There was no talking to him.

One time he was on the phone and I was supposed to have the boys that weekend. Gus was trying to tell me that I couldn't have them after all. He had plans. We started arguing and he was screaming on the phone at me and I was crying and screaming! I slammed that phone down. I was mad! I was mad at Gus, mad at God, mad at the world! I grabbed my car keys and I screamed to God… "You can't stop me God! If you aren't going to help me then I will help myself!"

Jim was at work and I called him and told him that I was going to go get my boys and if Gus tried to stop me I would beat the crap out of him or die trying. I hung up on Jim, got in my car and I started screaming at God… I was screaming "Is this what you want God? " I was saying things like, "If you aren't going to help me, fine I will do it without you!"

I was heading toward Gus's house and nothing was going to stop me! Well, nothing but God! I stopped at a red light and I was crying, screaming in the car and suddenly my car stalled! Died right there on the spot! I tried to restart it, but it wouldn't turn over. Cars were honking behind me and I was jerking the steering wheel and sobbing and I just collapsed into the seat of that car. Laid there in the middle of traffic and sobbed and sobbed and suddenly there was a man at my car door.

"Ma'am, you ok?" he asked, I just laid there crying and I looked at him and couldn't say a word, I was crying too hard. "Ma'am" he said again, "it will be okay, we will get your car started, can't be that bad" and he opened my car door and reached his hand in for me to take. I sat up and grabbed his hand; silly guy thought I was having a breakdown because my car stalled.

Being real gentle he said, "Do you want to pop your hood so I can take a look?" I looked at him for what seemed like a long time, but I know now was probably only seconds. "No, no you don't need to look," I whispered. "Nothing is wrong with my car," I said.
I remember looking up out the front window of the car; I remember snickering just a tiny bit, "You win God," I whispered. "I am so sorry Father," I choked out and then I put my hands on the keys and turned the car over. It started! The man was still there.

"I am okay now," I said to him. "You sure," he answered. "Yes, I was just mad at God, but even when we are being an ass, God still takes care of us," I snickered again. The man nodded and gently shut my door and I thanked him and drove home. When I got home Jim was there. He had left work to come comfort me and talk to me. He was so glad to see me. I told Jim what had happened.

Awhile later, I really had time to reflect on what had happened. There is no doubt in my mind that God intervened and saved my life that day. If I had made it to Gus as upset as I was I would have physically tried to hit him and he could have seriously hurt me. He also protected my boys from seeing me at my worst ever and from having to witness an ugly confrontation. And God had great compassion on me and he understood my anger and my hurt and my weakness!

I never argued with God like that again! Oh, there were times, and honestly are times when still I grow weary and hurt and get angry in my soul because I think God should fix the circumstances right away. I don't always understand His ways. I'm not supposed to. I have learned that a key ingredient to love is trust. If I say I love God then I have to trust Him in all things, in all ways. Because I am human I sometimes pout like a baby not getting her way, but my heavenly Father has my back. He always has.

REFLECTION

My relationship with God gives me the freedom to recognize my emotions and to express them to God. I can pour out my anger to Him and know He will not judge me but rather He will help me get to that better place. My emotions, like my skills and strengths, are from God. He included them in me when I was created. Some say they have left all their miseries and emotions at the foot of the cross; that they have laid it off on God. I can't because I believe they are mine, He gave them to me and if I was to lay them at the cross I would be missing very essential parts of who I am. Rather God stands by me and gives me the freedom and space to recognize my internal strengths. In that process I also gain insight into my unhealthy and destructive beliefs which need to change. I trust in God and in that trust I find the foundation for my restoration of my authentic self.

1993 Ed & Lily

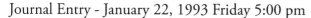

Journal Entry - January 22, 1993 Friday 5:00 pm

Today has been draining. Last night I had another memory. I'm real young, about 4 or 5 years old. Dad is wearing white boxer shorts and he is lying in bed. I am in bed with him and he is cuddling me. I'm lying on my side with my back to him. His penis has fallen out of the hole in his shorts. It is soft. He is humping my leg; sort of rubbing up against me. His penis is getting harder. I am pretending to be asleep. I wish he would stop and just let me sleep. That's all I remember. I don't remember what happens next. After remembering this I feel sick to my stomach; like I am going to vomit. I feel angry and sick and scared. The child in me wants to scream stop, please stop! Why? Oh God why? I feel emotionally drained like I had to relive the whole scene all over again.

I also remember an earlier time being little and being picked up and shaken violently and having my head banging against the wall. It is my mother who is shaking me. She wants me to stop crying but this makes me cry more. My feelings as a child were confused and mixed up. One minute my mom was loving and the next she was violent and out of control.

REFLECTION

As you can see on more than one occasion my body has automatically, naturally and unconsciously blocked the memory of the abuse as a means of saving me from further pain and suffering from the over-powering knowledge and emotions of the event. But that memory gap doesn't stop me from restoring myself. In fact, as Rebecca Born and Rachel Davis of Connections, A Safe Place have stated, total memory recall is not needed as it is not the details of the abuse that holds me back but rather it is the impact of the abuse. It is the impact that re-duces my ability to trust others, to feel safe around others, and to be intimate with others; it is the basis of my stinking thinking.

The details focus on what happened but in reality I need to focus on the impact and how it is affecting me now. As I grew in my self-awareness I realized that reliving the event (memory retrieval) was less helpful to my restoration than understanding the trauma. Rachel has told me of another client who has no memory of the abuse but has been able to restore herself by facing the fact that she has experienced trauma.

Accepting that there was trauma even without the details
is the most important step in healing! Rachel Davis

Because of the emotional weight of the abuse I needed to gain new coping skills to be able to face the details. I could not do it on my own; I wasn't prepared. Even now I need to recognize those emotions for what they are before they can take over. Thanks to God and my sup-port team I now have the skills to do that.

1994 RuthAnn

It was 1994 when Abe was starting sixth grade and Jack was in first grade. I was in my car driving and listening to *Focus on the Family* on the radio. The show was about a group of moms who got together weekly to pray for their children and their schools, peers, school staff, and that the schools be guided by biblical values and high moral principles. The group was called, "Moms in Touch" and there were groups all over the U.S. I felt drawn to them because of their belief that "every child needs a praying mom!"

If the school your children went to didn't have one, you could start one. I was very interested and called the middle school Abe was going to and Jack's elementary school to see if they had a Mom's in Touch group. Abe's school had one and Jack's school didn't have one. I joined the one at Abe's school and started one at Jack's.

I didn't know any of the moms at Jack's school. So I talked to the teachers and the principal and they gave me the names of some mom's and others gave me some names and soon Moms in Touch was formed for Jack's school. We met weekly taking turns in each other's homes and we prayed for our children, for their teachers, for their friends. I met some wonderful moms in that group and we continue to meet for many years.

When I called Abe's school to see if they had a Moms in Touch, they gave me the phone number of the lady who led it. I called her and went to their meeting. This was a huge step for me. I was now in two Christian women groups and was praying and having fellowship with them. Of course I didn't share too much of my background, just that the boys' father and I were divorced.

The ladies in both groups were so loving and kind. They weren't stand-offish or proud. They had nice homes and had only been married once and were the typical middle class families and I did pretty well in the groups until:

In Abe's school the leader of their Moms in Touch was RuthAnn. RuthAnn was a sweetheart of a person, warm and kind and gentle and thoughtful. She had the gift of hospitality and could make tea and cookies look like a splendid feast for a king.

Her house was warm and inviting and she was full of love. All the ladies drank tea. I didn't drink tea. I didn't even know how to make hot tea. I know that sounds crazy, but I hadn't exactly come from the tea and cookies background. When it was my turn to host Moms in Touch, all the ladies were invited to our apartment. Jim and I were living in a small two bedroom apartment at the time. I decided to serve tea in a fancy teapot that I had bought. When the time came for the meeting, I was excited to serve the ladies, especially RuthAnn. The meeting began and we were writing down prayer requests and I noticed that RuthAnn kept putting sugar and cream in her tea. She was trying her best to be kind and drink it. Finally I asked her if something was wrong with the tea.

RuthAnn kindly replied that it was a little strong. She asked me how I had made it. I showed her the box the tea came in. "How many of these bags did you put in the teapot?" she asked. "All of them," I replied.

Well that would have been bad enough if I had bought normal tea bags, but I had accidently picked up the family size tea bags. So each bag was big enough for about 6 cups of tea! I had put the whole box in the teapot! It was probably so strong it could have walked.

When I told RuthAnn that and she explained the difference in regular teabags and family size, we both started laughing. It was so funny. I might have been embarrassed for about a minute, but RuthAnn had a way of making a person feel comfortable.

I had attended many of the Mom's in Touch meetings before I realized that RuthAnn was a pastor's wife. She as so accepting and loving and easy going, I was shocked when I found out she was a pastor's wife. As the years went by, RuthAnn was always a very loving faithful friend. She lives in Pennsylvania now.

Editor Note: Mom's in Touch is known now as Mom's in Prayer International: www.momsinprayer.org

Alfonso B. Huckleberry Sr.

REFLECTION

I had this belief that church folks were above me. I mean Lily kept tell-ing me I wasn't good enough to be a Christian. After years of hearing that, I began to accept it and thus developed an unhealthy core belief that stayed with me. Rachel & Rebecca call it the power of agreement: in accepting what they say about me I give it power over me. I allowed others to label me and to treat me as they wanted to without regard for my true self. Like other bad beliefs and misdirections I needed to work on changing to the truth. It is only with the Truth that I am free.

LOVING ME

1998 Danielle

IN 1998 OUR daughter Danielle was born. When I became pregnant with Danielle, my mother told me that now things would be different! Jim would love Danielle more than Abe and Jack because she was his biological child. But nothing has been farther than the truth. Jim has never called Abe and Jack his step sons. He has always called them his sons. If someone asks Jim how many kids he has, he will always answer 3. He loves Abe and Jack as much as Danielle. He considers them his sons and he has never shown any difference in them.

Abe and Jack know the love Jim has for them. He has provided for them, cared for them, nurtured them, encouraged them, loved them - all the good things that a father does for his children. I know that God brought Jim and me together. Jim never judged me or the baggage that I carried. From the very beginning any baggage I held onto emotionally Jim helped me unpack!

2005 Church Conference

—⁓⁓—

For you were once darkness, but now you are light in the Lord. Live as children of light for the fruit of the light consists in all goodness, righteousness and truth and find out what pleases the Lord. Ephesians 5: 8-10

I WAS TAUGHT to associate God with duty and diligence. I was told that I would never be good enough to have a relationship with God. That is true; I will never be good enough to have a relationship with God. It is a very good thing that God doesn't require me to be good enough. There is not a scale big enough in the entire world to weigh enough goodness to stand up to the standard of a holy God. That is why God sent His Son, Jesus.

Because of my belief in Jesus as my Savior I am able to have a relationship with God. Having a relationship with anyone is a very serious thing. It took me many years to learn that. In fact, I do not talk of myself as having a specific church affiliation but that I am in a relationship with God.

When you have a relationship with a friend, a spouse, or with Jesus you have to work at it, that relationship requires your time. It requires your commitment, it requires your love and respect, and it requires truth. God freely gives us all these things and more. We should give these things to Him and others.

A few years ago our ladies group at church was going on a trip to Tennessee to a ladies' conference. Jim thought he would surprise me for my birthday and paid for my reservation to go on the trip with the ladies. When he told me what he had done, I became very upset. I couldn't go on a trip with a bunch of Church ladies! I couldn't share a room with a church lady! They were Christian ladies and I was... well I thought I wasn't good enough! Wasn't... holy enough! Wasn't... smart enough! I started crying and yelling at Jim. "Why would you do this? What made you think I would want to go?" Sure I love Christian music; I love to praise the Lord. Yes, I do listen to Christian speakers all the time and have read all their books, but not an overnight trip with a group of Christian ladies!

I don't know what Jim said to our church, but he cancelled my reservation and got our money back. We never talked about it again. Later in therapy I talked about it. What did I miss experiencing from not going on that trip? Surely I missed out on getting to know my church sisters better and a wonderfully fun experience. They missed out on getting to know me; getting to know who I am - a child of God, not a bad person. I was still stuck; stuck in believing that I was bad. I was full of shame.

REFLECTION

I have gotten better over the years in changing my belief system about myself but, it is still the most difficult obstacle for me. I still struggle with shame. I am so thankful that I have my counselor Sandy in my life and that I continue to seek truth - God's truth.

I have never been to a Christian women's conference with a group of church ladies yet. But I believe it can happen. Better yet I can picture in my mind, being a speaker at their conference! I can see myself talking to them about my abuse honestly, authentically and openly so that they can see that there is more to a person who has been abused then a just the abuse and trauma. I can offer hope for a better life. To live as children of the light we must believe we ARE children of the light. There is no condemnation as God's child.

2006 Brain Tumor #2

THE PROPHET ISAIAH wrote that the Lord comforts His people and has compassion on the afflicted. Isaiah 49:13

In December of 2006, I went in to have my second brain tumor surgery. About a year before I had been having a lot of headaches/migraines and went to see my doctor and because of my history (having a brain tumor before) he ordered a MRI.

I will never forget the call. The phone rang and I picked it up. It was Dr. Gossard and he told me that they had found a tumor on the right frontal area of the brain. He said that they were almost sure it was benign and gave me the number of a surgeon. The tumor was called meningioma with possible short term memory loss as a side effect which I continue to have today.

Jim was at work when I got the call. Danielle and the boys were at school. I put the phone down and my first thought was, "Why? Haven't I suffered enough Lord?" I began to list all the terrible things I had been through, like if you reached a certain number than surely you would be exempt from more.

But if that was the case, who would hold the measuring scale? Who would determine that surely this or that person had suffered enough in this life and shouldn't have more bestowed upon them. If that was the case we would all sit around comparing our heartaches, our sorrows and we each would swear that certainly our suffering outweigh the other's and therefore we should have no more!

I think the simple truth is exactly what God says it is in the Bible: in this world we all will have sufferings. There is no avoiding it, no getting around it and only one way through it. The only way to get through it is to allow the hand of God to hold yours and to allow Him to lead you through it one step, one minute, one breathe at a time.

Of course we don't like that solution because we want God to take it all away. We don't want to feel the pain, the agony, it hurts too badly, it is too overwhelming or so it seems. But the Bible goes on to say yes you will have sufferings in this world but fear not for "I have overcome the world." (John 16:33) What does that mean? I have found that in every painful life situation, no matter how awful, how gut wrenching it was, there was always this amazing love that sustained me. It was God's love. How else can I explain how I got through each situation? How else could I be still standing today and still receiving God's grace and love on a daily basis? I believe that God's love has overcome the world. Bring it on! There is no way any evil against us can prosper! God's love is too strong, too pure, too genuine, and too beautiful to not overcome the pain and suffering of this world! Yes the sufferings of this world hurt, oh my how they hurt. But the love of God embraces us, carries us, it makes all things new. It is a restoring love, a healing love, an endless love.

So now I had a brain tumor and I thought it unfair. Yes I did in the moment of my weakness and pain, but I also knew that God's love was strong enough and that was what I had to hold on to.

It took a while for the news to sink in. I had a benign meningioma which was growing and needed to get out. I could start having seizures if I just left it in there to grow and fester much like the fear, hurt, anger that we carry when we go through a tremendous trial. If we leave all those feelings inside us to grow and fester which they will then they will become far more deadly than any trial we will ever face.

Because of where the tumor was located the surgeon had told me that it could affect my short term memory. I could wake up and not remember Jim or my kids' names. They really didn't know until they got in there. I had an amazing group of loving, supporting friends who were standing with me. My friend Ann was battling cancer at the same time. My brain surgery was scheduled to take place in December 2006. I went to visit Ann at her house right before Thanksgiving. She was wearing a wig and was small and frail. I brought us lunch and we talked like nothing was going on. Maybe we both were pretending that I wasn't going to have brain surgery in a few weeks and that she wasn't terminally ill. We talked about Thanksgiving and Ann mentioned that she wanted a quiet Thanksgiving with her kids. Ann had a nurse coming in and I talked to her about my fear of my upcoming surgery.

Looking back now I wish I held her, I wish I had fallen on my knees and told her how much her love meant to me. I wish I said so many things. But maybe it was better this way. She knew she was dying and she couldn't tell me. She couldn't hurt me. And I guess I knew too, but I was in so much denial. I just always wanted Ann to be in my life. I couldn't think of a day without her.

I had my brain surgery. Ann didn't come to the hospital. I was so medicated that I didn't think anything about it at the time. I received some beautiful flowers from Ann with a card that said "'I hope you are feeling better every day' Love, Ann." Three weeks after my brain tumor surgery my beloved Ann died. Her daughter called me and told me. I went to her services with a scarf tied around my head to hide the bandages. I leaned on Jim to walk from the car to the church. The service was beautiful. I never got to say good bye to Ann. Not really. For a long time I resented that. I wanted to hold her hand as she left this earth to go to her home in Heaven, but Ann didn't want that. I was recovering from brain surgery and Ann knew that watching her die, or saying good bye would have been too much for me. I think even in her death she was protecting me.

I have never gone to Ann's grave. I just haven't been able to. I know she isn't there. That it is just a memorial, a place to remember her. But I carry our memories in my heart every day and I see her in me, the way she touched my life, the way she gave to me so I could grow and become a better person. I keep the little card that was attached to the flowers she sent me in my office at home on a bulletin board. "'Hope you are feeling better every day', Love Ann." So simple was the message. But that was her wish for me, to grow better, be better, live better, and feel better every day. That is what I try to do.

And we know that God causes everything to work together for the good of those who love God and are called according to his purpose for them. Romans 8:28

REFLECTION

My relationship with Ann was a gift from God. No one can ever convince me otherwise. A senior citizen, a lady with an affluent background hospitalized for severe depression and me, in my early 30's from poverty and despair sharing a room! What a place to meet. What a beginning to a life changing relationship. What a gift from God. Sometimes I wonder what that above Romans verse means. Then I smile because I lived that Bible verse in the midst of my pain, in the midst of my depression, in the midst of despair He gave me Ann. And it was very good! Danielle, my daughter, recently wrote a paper on death for her high school class. Like the colors and the brush strokes that make a masterpiece, my memories of Ann are sharp, vivid, alive, striking and always with me. Danielle wrote that death is like the artist's signature at the bottom of the work. It is God's way of saying this life, this masterpiece will live forever.

After my brain tumor surgery and Ann's death, I slowly began to recover. I did have a little short term memory loss and still do, but it was not too bad at all. I just use a lot of sticky notes!

The Museum of the Universe

IMAGINE WALKING INTO an art museum filled with nothing but blank canvases. As you walk through the halls you see other people walking around and as you enter one particular room you realize that some visitors have started painting on the canvases. You wander around for a while, watching them work. Eventually someone hands you a set of paints and guides you to a blank canvas with your name written next to it. They leave you with one instruction, paint something, anything, but make sure it's worth your time, because you only have the one canvas.

This scenario seems relatively simple, uncomplicated and easy to understand, yet I propose it can be used to answer one of the most complex questions ever asked, and may be used to define one of the most misunderstood words in any language. That word is "life." And I believe that life can be defined as the opportunity given to all, but accepted by few. It is the chance that we are all awarded to leave our mark on the world. Life is our chance to add a piece of priceless art to the Museum of the Universe. Life is a series of moments strung together in a tangled mess. The order doesn't matter as much as some people think; only the moments do. These moments are like brushstrokes in an impressionist painting: little dots that are insignificant by themselves, but that are invaluable to the formation of the bigger picture. Some of the dots are bigger than others, some stand out from the rest, and some just fill in the background, but they are all important to the work.

Taylor Schreiber

PART TWO

On occasion the brushstrokes are shaky, and certain dots aren't pleasing to look at. Sometimes attempts are made to cover these mistakes up, but in the end one only succeeds in attracting more attention to the blemish. Eventually, the best artists learn to just accept mistakes, and to move on, to continue painting. This is the way that it is with life, except that even fewer people remember to continue living beyond a past failure. This is why some paintings in the Museum of the Universe are half- finished; their artists never moved on to the next stroke.

When you find yourself painting in this museum it can be hard not to look at the way other people are painting their canvases. You might try to mimic another person's art, and that's okay, a lot of people do that, and often they produce the most beautiful and popular paintings. It is important to note, however, that if every painting's the same, then there's no need for a museum. If every person lives their life the same way, then there's no need for a universe. The word, "life" means something different for each human being. You were not born to be Van Gogh, Vermeer, or Da Vinci. You were born to be you.

Some people in life are born with more privileges than others, think of this as having more paints and more brushes to use. Having these privileges can sometimes make it easier to make a masterpiece, but not always. Certain masters have been known to do more with one color of paint and their fingertips, than others have done with twenty colors and brush. Life is not a contest over who can gather the best materials; rather it is a journey to see what you can make with what you've been given.

I've spoken much about canvases and paintings and I want to make sure that I clarify something. Life is not a canvas, or a piece of art. Life is the *opportunity* to use a canvas; it is the *chance* to make a piece of art. This is a comforting point of view because it renders death irrelevant. Oftentimes people make the mistake of assuming that life is a straight line, an experience with a clear beginning and end. It is because of this mistake that people fear death so much. They believe that it is the end of all things, but they are greatly mistaken. Death is not the end, not at all. Death is only the signature on the painting.

A masterpiece is not struck meaningless when it is signed; in contrast, it is given even more value. In much the same way life is not ended by death, in contrast, life is showcased by it. If a painting is beautiful, unique, or powerful enough then it does not end once the signature is painted. It is hung in a museum for all to see and centuries after it was made it is still talked about and praised. But this only happens in the case of the greatest paintings.

And now to answer those ancient questions all men have asked. The definition of life? Life is the only chance you are given to create a masterpiece. The meaning? To create the most extraordinary masterpiece you can, one that will hang in the Museum of the Universe for centuries, even after you've signed it away.

Danielle Watkins, 2015

2007 Ed

MY DAD DIED on Nov. 5th 2007. He was 83 years old. He died laying in his nursing home near his birth home of Eubanks, Ky.

I am not sure what is listed as the cause of his death. He had been in a kind of vegetated state for a couple years prior to his death. My husband Jim and I had visited him a couple times. Once my friend Paula took me to visit him; I don't know if he knew me. He couldn't talk. He just laid there flat on his back, staring at the ceiling: unable to speak, unable to move. A feeding tube was keeping him alive.

I never would wish that kind of death on anyone. When I saw him lying there helpless, I thought of the times in my life that I felt helpless, especially by his hands. It wasn't a revengeful thought or even anger, it was just extreme sadness. If I would have been given the power to touch him and restore him to health I would have. Not because I am of noble character, ha…..no not that at all. But because of the Holy Spirit who dwells inside of me I didn't desire revenge. I simply didn't want revenge; I didn't want to see him lay there like that. Vengeance is mine sayeth the Lord. I knew what he was feeling. He was scared, helpless, and uncertain I knew exactly those feelings. I had experienced all of those feelings at his hands. I wouldn't wish those feelings on my worst enemy and there he laid like that for years… in many ways my worst enemy.

I cried at my dad's funeral. I cried for everything lost. Lost innocence, lost love, lost time, lost peace… I cried tears of anger and remorse, love and hate and I left those tears there at his grave.

2009 Danielle

IN OCTOBER OF 2009, Danielle had to have a very serious back surgery. She had scoliosis and her spine had grown like the letter "S." It was getting so bad that there was risk of the spine moving against vital organs. She was 11 years old in sixth grade and Jim and I were told that we couldn't put off the surgery any longer.

She went into the hospital on 10/2/09 and came home on 10/8/09. Jim and I spend every day and every night at the hospital with her. We slept in the room with her. The surgery took 7 hours to perform and she ended up having 16 screws in her back and 2 metal rods.

Seeing your child go through something like that is awful; it was a very difficult time in our marriage! One day a friend called me and I stepped out in the hall and sobbed. I didn't want Danielle to see me crying. Slowly she sat up and then longer each day and then with a walker she started taking a few steps in the hallway. She came home with a walker and she did not return to school until January. She had a tutor.

All of our friends and church family were amazing during this time! They covered us in prayer and their love, prayers and comfort got us all through. New Hope Community Church where Jim and I still attend had a great big box of goodies that everyone made for Danielle. Coloring books, crayons, stuff animals, balloons, craft kits all kinds of goodies. When we brought Danielle home our whole dining room table was covered with flowers, cards, presents, stuff animals and etc. for Danielle. It was an over whelming show of love, Jim and I were so grateful. Our little girl had pulled through surgery and was on the road to recovery.

2010 Vertigo Attack

In August of 2010, I went school shopping with Danielle. We spent the day buying her school clothes for the upcoming school year and buying her school supplies. I was feeling fine. That night I was getting ready for bed and I told Jim that I felt funny. He asked me what funny meant. I just kept saying, I feel funny, like something just wasn't right. It was like I was disconnected, my head felt weird and then suddenly I started having a severe vertigo attack. The room was really spinning and I was vomiting and I didn't know what was happening. I thought maybe I had another brain tumor or something was wrong with where they had done the surgery. I had four screws in my skull and I didn't know how those things were, I just knew something was really wrong.

Jim called the life squad and my friend Paula came over and stayed with Danielle. My head wouldn't stop spinning, my speech was a little slurred and I was vomiting. They gave me an IV in the squad for nausea. When I got to the hospital they told me I was having a severe vertigo attack. They gave me something in my IV to stop it. Although it made it a lot better it didn't make the vertigo completely go away. I stayed 6 days in the hospital. I kept having vertigo attacks, one after another. They would give me something to stop it, it would slow down, sometimes go away and then a little while later it would come back strong as ever! It was awful.

They sent me home when they got the vertigo calmed enough to only be extremely light headed instead of a full spinning motion. After 6 days in the hospital, I was in a wheel chair. This started a terrible, long journey. The good news was there were no more tumors, bad news was, something was badly wrong and they were trying to find out what. I was also shaking uncontrollably. My speech was a little slurred and I couldn't concentrate at all. One doctor thought for sure that I was displaying signs of MS and sent me to a specialist. He was so convinced that I had MS that I was trying to prepare myself for living with MS for the rest of my life.

I had another MRI and CAT scan and so many tests I can't even count them all. I did have legions on my brain and upper neck like MS, but this specialist said that I would have them all down my spine if it was MS. Later another neurologist specialist had argued that wasn't necessary true.

I was doing balance therapy and was still in a wheel chair. I couldn't walk without assistance. I was having vertigo attacks either several times a day or a few a day, but every day. My hands shook and I could barely write. My concentration level was gone. I just wanted to know what was going on, what I had and if they could treat it. More specialists. In fact I went to 3 different neurologists/surgeons and 3 different ENTS.

For two years I couldn't drive. I did manage to go from the wheel chair to a walker but, I was still very dependent on Jim for my care and well-being. I was so frustrated and depressed. I went from an active working full-time woman to a disabled one that couldn't walk without the aid of a walker, couldn't drive at all anymore and was unable to work at all.

REFLECTION

The virus that attacked my nervous system left me physically crippled. The abuse left me emotionally crippled. I hate my physical limitations but my illness made me vulnerable and I realized that I had so much more healing to do. I have fought them both and I will continue to fight every day of my life. It is that important. But I cannot fight on my own. Only through the love of Christ can I be victorious warrior.

I can do all things through him who gives me strength.
Philippians 4:13

LOVING ME

2010 Jim

MY HUSBAND JIM was a saint. My friends were praying and loving me and trying their best to comfort me. I was still going to balance therapy and seeing my doctor regularly. I started seeing a therapist because I knew I was depressed and sad and mad and everything all at the same time. I noticed that I was really scared. I was totally dependent on Jim and that scared me to death! Because deep inside I still had abandonment issues, I still feared Jim would leave me, I still had trust issues, I thought I couldn't trust Jim's vow he made to love me though better or worse. I had panic attacks and the nightmares started coming. Nightmares of long ago and memories began to assault me.

Over the years I had went to counseling and groups and done a lot to heal myself of the abuse that had taken place in my past, but I did what I needed to do to get through or what I thought had healed me enough. But there were fears and emotions buried deep inside of me caused from my past experiences and I had tried so hard to bury them. Now I was sick and not independent and I needed Jim and those emotions, that stinking thinking, started surfacing and I knew that my physical ailments were not the only thing that needed to heal. I had a lot more spiritual and emotional healing to do.

I was sent to Dr. Hobekia who at the time was the top neurologist and head specialist in Cincinnati. He had been a specialist for a long, long time. I liked him immediately. He was tough and forthright and he did every test known to man on me (well that is what it seemed like at the time). I would try to walk on this machine while the ground became uneven and moved up and down hills, I was put on a table and made to have vertigo and the waves in my head were measured. I had things attached to me and was monitored and measured and so on and so forth. I hated it, but I felt like at least this doctor was going to get to the bottom of things and help me. I was walking with a cane now. I had gone from a wheelchair to a walker to a cane. I was always light headed, that feeling never left. The shaking would subside and only on occasions revisit me. I still wasn't allowed to drive and basically I couldn't walk unless someone was babysitting me. Vertigo still came almost daily, but not several times a day and not always severe.

I started a blessing book. I was so afraid that I would give up and lose my faith. I was weary, tired of suffering and I was angry. I thought if I started a blessing book, one that I would make myself write in it every day and I make myself write down at least three things I was thankful for each day. Three things would help me not to get so depressed and help me to hang on to my faith.

There were days when I literally had to force myself to write in that blessing book. I would be mad or discouraged and I didn't want to count my blessings, I didn't want to be thankful. I had enough suffering and yet I would write in it. It became a daily habit. I wrote in it every day and soon I would be writing five things, seven, ten, sometimes so many, I would just keep writing. And to this day I still write in it. I have filled many a notebook writing down my blessings and I have over eleven thousand blessings written down. Sometimes it will be a beautiful sunset or a robin sitting on a branch other days it was I walked to the bathroom by myself. One day Jim took me to an abandoned parking lot and he let me drive. I drove about 20 feet and I had to stop. I cried and cried and when I got home I wrote in my blessing book, "Today I drove!"

I have kept the habit of writing in my blessing book even today because I have learned how to be thankful for the smallest thing to the biggest miracle. I have learned how to see God in sunsets and blooming flowers and the smiles of strangers and the kindness of friends and I have learned that everything and every day is a gift from God. Really! It is.

At the end of all the testing Dr. Hobekia thought that a virus had caused an erosion of inner ear surfaces which affects balance and the virus had done nerve damage. It couldn't be cured and my symptoms could be managed but never ever go away. I then lost 50% of my hearing in my right ear.

I am trying to be very careful when writing about this time in my life. I want this book to be about hope and encouragement and God's love and not about bitterness or hatred. I understand now that to some of my family I will always wear the labels that were given to me long ago. I will always be the liar, over dramatic, the attention seeker, and the faker. It was easier for them long ago to label me with those destructive titles and much easier on them if they kept them on me. I think that in the family's own dysfunctional way, they believe those labels of me. It is the lies that we all believe growing up in an abusive home and situations that can destroy us and unless one is willing to seek help, heal, seek love and grow then they can never see truth. I have explained how those labels came to be. My actions were not always true or wise but, I didn't deserve to be branded, no one does. The scarlet letters, the name calling, the fingers pointing are all dysfunctional traits that are taught and passed down generation to generation unless someone breaks the cycle. For me, my husband and the kids the cycle has stopped! I no longer live in that cycle and I don't allow it in my life. So during this journey there were those who said I was faking all of this. There were those that said it wasn't that bad. There were even those who said I was a lazy bum who didn't work and used friends when my friends threw a fundraiser to buy me a $1,800.00 hearing aid that insurance wouldn't pay for. Yes, they said those things to me. Hopefully you, my reader, can feel the hurt inside me as it pours out from these words. I have let it out; now I must let it go! I do not agree with them and their labels have no power over me. I will not carry that shame; I will not carry that message.

2012 Lily

WHEN MOM COULDN'T care for herself, she lived with my two brothers and sister. They took turns having her live with them. I refused to have her live with me. It wasn't because I was mad or bitter or to be spiteful, I was different and I didn't want my daughter expose to her "wit" on a daily basis.

I would buy mom clothes, I would buy her groceries, I even offered to pay for any Assisted Living she might need, but she wasn't living with me. My mom liked to be funny when she was around people. She was in her 80's and would flip people the finger, joking around. Anything went. Dirty jokes and sexual jokes, flipping the finger, and she was very blunt!!! She had always said whatever was on her mind to whomever she wanted and even in her 80's she still did. She would call someone a whore or tell them they dressed as a slut, whatever she wanted to say.

My brothers, sister, nieces and nephews thought she was a riot! So funny! For the most part I thought she was obnoxious. Our sons were grown and out of our house, but our daughter was still young and living at home. No way was I going to expose her to mom's humor. (That is what the family called it) I got a lot of grief from family members for not allowing her to live with me.

As I write this, a few days ago was the anniversary of my mother's death. My mom died Sept. 24th 2012. She died lying in her bed at my sister's home where she was living at the time. All of her children were with her. She was 87 years old.

The emotions were raw that night. It was hard to say good bye. I loved her, I still love her. I had come to peace with our battles, I had forgiven her even though I can't remember a time that she ever said she was sorry to me. I had long ago apologized to her for any hurt I had caused her and I sincerely meant it.

There was a part of me that longed to hear her voice those too powerful words "I'm sorry." I try to be sincerely sorry and to apologize when I hurt someone. I try really hard to learn from my mistakes and not repeat them. Sometimes I am a quick learner, other times not so much.

I do know that there is power in those two little words "I'm sorry." Confessing, turning away from and trying harder should go hand in hand with a sincere apology.

My sister and I had a disagreement the night mom died. I love my sister. I always have. When I look at Sissy I see a wounded soul that radiates a garden of beauty in spite of her wounds. Because of the deep wounds left to never completely heal inside of her, she hasn't been freed to fully grow in all the remarkable ways God has intended for her. She is gentle and creative and loving. She is also very scared and timid and hurt. She is the illustration of how beautiful wild flowers can still grow among the weeds and it leaves you wondering just how much more majestic those wild flowers would be if the weeds were to be removed.

Sissy and I argued over where mom was to be buried. Mom hadn't left a will or written down any final wishes. Sissy wanted mom buried in a small country town, I wanted mom buried in a local graveyard nearby. In the end mom got buried where Sissy wanted in the country.

When I look back at it now, it seems ironic that mom was somehow putting Sissy and I at odds against each other even in her death. My mom was very good at manipulation, especially with Sissy and me.

I don't visit mom's grave much: her birthday and around Christmas. It is a little drive from my house; but mostly, I'm just not a big grave side visitor. I don't mean to be cold. I know Sissy does a great job of maintaining mom's grave. Sissy has always taken care of mom. She received way too much of the pain and abuse and maybe she just couldn't give herself permission to stop taking care of mom even in death.

When I think of my mom now, I try real hard to remember the good times, the funny, silly her.

REFLECTION

I have begun to set boundaries that help me. Setting boundaries frees me from the entanglements of being lost in someone else's control and influence. I can demand the respect I deserve and be treated as I should be. In so doing I protect my identity and my rights.

Learning how to take better care of myself emotionally has not been easy. In the past I wanted love so bad that I got myself into unhealthy relationships or didn't set boundaries in unhealthy relationships. Of course when I was a child I couldn't do anything about it. As an adult it took me a while to learn what was healthy and what wasn't. I had lived in dysfunction for so long, that was all I knew. Now I am a much healthier adult (emotionally) so I have learned how to set boundaries. I have learned to identify what is a healthy relationship and what isn't.

But setting the boundaries can be painful and frustrating. Not allowing people you love to hurt you can be painful because you want them to love you in a healthy way, but you can't make them. You want anyone you have a relationship with to be respectful of your feelings, but you can't make them be respectful. You can only set the boundary. You can only say this has to stop or we can't have a relationship and that is a very hard thing for me. The great news is I can do this! I can and have done this now. I have lost some relationships and that hurt because I loved them. But a toxic relationship is poisonous to my soul. It will take and take from me until I am a shell with nothing left to give. So standing up for me, taking care of myself isn't being selfish or mean. It is loving myself in a good, healthy way. I might lose a relationship; if I do then it is safe to say it was toxic for me anyway. And if I don't lose a relationship, then I will gain respect and love.

Letting someone know in a non-argumentative way that what they said or did hurt me is important. It is the beginning of loving me. I have lived in shame all my life. I don't want to live there anymore, so I must take up for myself. I must love myself as a child of God. Allowing someone to continue to hurt me emotionally, physically, any way is allowing someone to continually hurt a child of God's!

I have a lot of growing still to do in this area, but I am better at it than I was yesterday and tomorrow I will be even better at it.

2013 Kent

IN THE SUMMER of 2013 my son Jack came home for good from the Marines, after serving five years. Jim and I were so very proud of him. We wanted to throw him a huge welcome home party. We invited all of Jack's friends, my family and Jim's family; our closest friends. I wanted the typical family event; all of us together celebrating Jack's return.

My oldest brother Kent has always been the only real father figure I have ever had. He is almost 15 years older than me. He got married the first time very young. He and his wife Joy lived with my mother, my little brother Joe and me until they divorced when I was in fourth grade. Joy and Kent provided for us financially. At the time my mother didn't work. Kent and Joy made our birthdays and Christmases for Joe and me.

I always longed Kent's approval. I also wanted someone to be proud of me.

Jim and I planned a great welcome home party for Jack. I wanted Kent and his present wife Reba to come. Kent owns a fitness center. We don't see him very often, hardly ever. Kent is very devoted to his business and is very business orientated. I asked Kent if he could please come to Jack's party. I knew he had people that work for him. But he said he couldn't leave the gym. He became very agitated.

I was still very weak and having a lot of physical problems at the time. My friends had set up a fund raiser to pay for a hearing aid I needed. I had lost 50% of my hearing in my right ear. They posted it on Facebook. They contacted family and friends letting them know about the fundraiser. My family didn't give.

While I was on the phone trying to persuade Kent to come to Jack's party, he became very irate with me. He started raising his voice and yelled at me. "I told you I am working at the gym that day. I am not coming to the party. Do you think Jack gives a shit if some old uncle is there or not? Unlike you, who sits on her ass, I work to pay my bills. I work so if I need a hearing aid, I can buy one! I don't have to bum off friends!"

I was sobbing! Kent thought I was a lazy bum that didn't work. I couldn't even talk I was crying so hard. I hung up the phone and fell to the floor crying. All those old labels came back in my mind.

Never mind that for over a year I hadn't been able to walk on a daily basis. Never mind that I was using a wheelchair or a walker on a regular basis. I wasn't allowed or able to drive. It would be almost 3 years before I was well enough to drive again and even now never by myself and only on short trips.

My friends saw how I struggled. Insurance wouldn't pay for my hearing aid. Because of their love and kindness I now have a hearing aid and can hear.

Jack had a great party in spite of this incident. I didn't tell Jack anything about what Kent had said. I called Kent after that and apologized. Kent did say he was sorry too. He tried to make light of what he said, but again he told me that I did need to get a job.

The little girl in me longed desperately for the happy family. I longed for their attention, their praise. I longed for a lot of things. BUT I have learned that sometimes because of unhealthy family dynamics, boundaries have to be made. I get my love and support from my husband Jim, from my kids and from friends who believe in me. I have to stop expecting my siblings and many others in my family to be able to give me what I longed for. They are not in the same place I am.

If you were to talk to them today you would hear things about me like, well she has been married so many times! She did get pregnant as a teenager! She fakes her illnesses. Remember the time she was 12 and she got hurt on a bike accident but stopped crying when the nice firefighter helped her! A Christian! Her? Do you know her past? On and on.........I have heard it all my life. I have worn the labels, I still fight the shame. But I don't want to believe that about myself. I can see where I have been, I know what has happened to me, and I still live with a chronic illness. But it is not my identity. It is not who I am. I am God's daughter. I am saved by amazing grace. I am healed and forgiven and I forgive those who trespassed against me. I want to give others hope. I want the abuse of children to stop! I want domestic violence to end! I can do all that God strengthens me to do. I can keep pressing on. I can't stop the violence or the abuse, but I can offer hope. I love my sister Sissy. I grieve that even today she is unable to shop on her own, to do ordinary little things like buy milk, get gas or even drive herself. She admits to having been abused by our uncle and can tell me horrible things done to her and me when I was too young to remember. But, she can't free herself, she can't move beyond. I can offer love and I can offer my story..........to help Sissy and others heal.

REFLECTION

It is the tragic reality of life that children are unable to process their abuse, their trauma. They don't have the mental capacity to move forward. The mind spends so much time defending and protecting that the child's growth stops at that age, at that level. In many ways my sister and brothers have not gotten past the age they were when the abuse occurred either directly to my sister or indirectly to my brothers. It is almost as if they need to be "reparented," to have a loving adult show them, train them on the skills they failed to develop.

John Martino

2014 Sandy

Today I had an appointment with Sandy, my counselor. She is an amazing Christian counselor and friend. She read a part of the article out of her "Leadership Journal" today. John Ortberg (a pastor/speaker/scientist) who has written several books wrote an article in Leadership Journal magazine on the brain and brain development and how the frontal area of the brain is the last to develop and that area is the one that helps us make decisions and choices. It said that science now knows that, that part of the brain does NOT develop until early to mid-twenties. It was very interesting what she read of it.

Her reason in reading it was because I continue to carry the blame for the sexual abuse because I did not tell anyone. She is trying to help me heal from that lie. So her argument is a 13, 14 year old girl is not capable of making wise decisions in that kind of situation and is very easily manipulated.

Sandy also shared a very good parable today which I loved. It goes like this:

> There once was a very old, toothless lion. He still had to hunt for his food and do his part - he would stand in front of the hippos or rhinos and he would roar this very loud, scary roar! The hippos hearing this scary roar ran away from it and straight

into a pack of lions that were waiting for them. If the hippos had ran toward the scary roar they would had been safe.

Adults heal the most when they face what they fear the most! Don't run from the roar! Meaning even though writing this book and digging up bad memories and going to counseling and the Connections support group can seem very scary, if I don't quit and if I face the roar I will heal! I face the roar every day. I refuse not to not face it! Facing it is healing! I also feel very shameful for the broken relationships / divorces I have had. But I learned today the top 5 characteristics of a person who has been either verbally abused, physical abused, sexually abused or all 3. They go a long way in explaining my behavior for so long:

Promiscuity
Broken relationships
Unplanned pregnancy or abortions
Drugs, alcohol addictions
Spiritual brokenness

If someone comes into a counselor's office with one or more of these traits in their past, the counselor can usually know that there has been abuse in this person's past. Much like if a woman had a husband that was gone all hours of the night, traveled a lot, never let her see his cell phone; it would probably be safe to bet he is having an affair. Today was a very helpful day in counseling.

REFLECTION

My fears are strongest where I have the least power to control or change the situation. Gavin DeBecker in *The Gift of Fear* writes that what one fears is usually not what one thinks they fear. For example the person that is afraid of water and swimming is actually afraid of drowning.

Point number two is the fact you fear something means it has not happened. If it hasn't happened then you have the power and time to change it.

2014 *Loving Me* Effect

DECEMBER 21, 2014 by John Hunt

Vicki's words resonate with others. Following the inclusion of "*Loving Me*" *(the poem)* on The Jason William Hunt Foundation's website we received a request for aid from a mother whose son was battling his own demons. She had been to the website and wrote

> *Thank you for posting the beautiful poem on the Mission page—I plan on sending it to my son in his next letter. It puts the words that I have tried to express in a much better way than I have stated to him.*

I shared this email with Vicki and she responded

> *Thank you John for sharing that note, it made me cry. Like you, I have wanted my sorrow to be used for someone else's joy. I don't know if I said that right, but you know what I mean. If our pain can make a difference in another's person life, then well… it had a purpose. I pray over our book every night.*

2015 Connections: A Safe Place

I WENT TO my Connections support group last night and we did a worksheet. I have attached the worksheet so you can look at it. It was a very difficult session, but eye opening. The group is a big help in healing the sexually abused. The spaces are the ones I filled in and how I view myself. I am still very shaky today and having difficulty physically so I hope I sent this right. I will be sending you another document as well.

[See "Connections Worksheet #1 and #2" in back of book]

As you can see the work we do digs very deep. These make us look at ourselves differently and in a good positive way. The drawing, my Portrayal of Resistance, represents all the people who tried to destroy me and told me I was bad or wouldn't amount to anything. I am hiding behind the wall because it feels safe. No more hiding! I am confronting the lies! I hid in the dark for a long time. I want to live in the light and stay in the light.

REFLECTION

I have been taught for so long all that is bad with me that it is hard to cling to, let alone recognize, what is good in me. It is hard because I am just now finding out what is good, what is creative, what is positive in me. I constantly jump to the negative about me. I need to learn to self-talk myself into better and healthier thinking. I need to stop this stinking thinking!

If a child is abused, as I was, has problems trusting others, has never been taught anything positive about oneself, grew up in an unstable home life, has fears of the unknown and fears believing in something new then the wall gets taller and stronger; while the reasons, the causes for the disassociations multiply. And then the excuses grow: fear, feelings of guilt and shame, unwillingness, difficulty in taking responsibility for healing, for doing what needs to be done to heal. It is hard, hard work. Fear is my biggest battle. I always think I will fail or fear that I will. The good thing is I recognize it now: I refuse to give up! I face it. God makes all things new! Me, I'm new! New Beginnings! New Today! New Tomorrow! Keeping secrets doesn't bring healing or change! Change and healing start from being open and recognizing the truth, even when the truth is ugly.

2015 Under the Stars Shoppe

———— ∿ ————

IN JERIMIAH 29:11 God says, *I know the plans I have for you.* Sometimes it may seem like that quote couldn't possibly be true, but then on some days like this day in Feb. I know that it is true and I can see how God had it planned and worked it out. In Feb. of 2015 Jim and I were in Batavia, Ohio running an errand for a friend. We couldn't find our way to the place we were looking for. We stopped at a building and saw a man sitting at a counter inside. We went inside to ask for directions.

When we went inside a very nice man named Matt was sitting at the counter of a somewhat empty building. We ask him for directions and started talking to him. That brief introduction was the beginning of me being able to open my store Under the Stars. In March the downstairs of that building would become home to a beautiful art gallery/store of mine and thanks to Matt's and his wife Faith's kindness a whole new exciting, wonderful chapter of my life has begun.

> *Be not forgetful to entertain strangers; for thereby some have entertained angels unawares.* Hebrews 13:2

Now I know that neither Matt nor Faith are Heavenly angels, but when a person who is filled with the love of Christ in their heart does an act of kindness to a stranger the power that is felt is definitely on an angelic scale! It can be life changing! God's love can be reflected through His people. Sometimes it can be the only light a person sees.

Opening **Under the Stars** has been a gift from God and He used two kind strangers to help make it happen.

2015 Meltdown

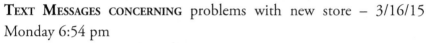

TEXT MESSAGES CONCERNING problems with new store – 3/16/15
Monday 6:54 pm

Having a terrible night! So frustrating. I won't go in to it all right now, but I could really use some prayers. You think one thing life would have taught me is not to be so gullible. Just wanted you and friends to pray. I have to give it to God and see what his will for me is. I am just frustrated and disappointed. Thanks for praying,

3/16/15 Monday 8:14 pm

I am sitting in a parking lot crying my eyes out. I am so upset. I am trying to talk to God but I think my hurt and anger is getting in the way. I am typing this on my phone so I hope you can read it. I shouldn't be driving at night, but I had to. I just am so angry! Angry at Lily and Ed for being such awful parents, angry at the world and probably at myself most of all. I feel like such a failure.

3/16/15 Monday 8:38 pm

Needed to have a pity party and a good cry but not in front of Danielle. We have a one level, very small house. If someone is upset everyone knows it.

Alfonso B. Huckleberry Sr.

3/16/15 Monday 9:01 pm

I am fine. Sometimes you just gotta have a good cry and then pick yourself up again and go on. I just didn't want Danielle to see me having a meltdown. Thanks for praying. And listening. I appreciate it. I will email you some more for the book tomorrow. Tomorrow is my birthday! Thanks again

REFLECTION

I am a very sensitive person. Because of my low self-esteem I take things too personally sometimes. When I wrote this I let fear control my emotions. Sometimes I don't catch myself at this destructive thinking until after the fact. I look back and think, *REALLY!!* I am working on trying not to be so sensitive.

But I also learn and see how old feelings surface. Constantly I ask for God's help, his guidance and I work at being better. That old saying – you can't see the forest from the trees – is true. I am learning how to react, how to be the kind of person God intended me to be. I pick myself up when I fall and it is **never** by my own strength. It is through Christ who strengthens me.

2015 Grand Opening

Text Message April 18, 2015 Saturday 6:18 pm

John & Rosemarie, thank you for coming today. I invited my brothers, my sisters, my cousins…not one person from my family showed up. And even though it shouldn't it still hurts.

Journal Entry May 19, 2015

Today I am sitting in my store. This is a new adventure for me. In spite of health problems, in spite of circumstances, God literally opened a door for me. I think what needs to be remembered is when God opens a door; we still have to walk through it. I have walked through a lot of doors that I forced open myself. Never giving any thought to why they were so hard to open in the first place. Looking back now, realizing they were closed for a reason.

It is an easy thing for me to say I love the Lord. Trust, is not so easy for me. That is a sad but transparent statement of who I was, but not on who I am becoming. I trust more. Letting go of what is not mine to own. I am tired of chasing circumstances or relationships I cannot fix I just want to walk hand in hand with the Lord. I want to be trusting in a sincere, pure love.

So I sit here. Physically the pain comes; concentration can be close to impossible some days. Just yesterday I had to use the walker to help me balance/ walk. But my spirit dances. It dances in the freedom that comes from living in the light.

My tears are real, my fears are real, and sometimes I am an ugly dragon that throws out fire, trying to consume all that hurts me. But what is really cool, is that those times of being a dragon are coming fewer and fewer and more and more I am able to let God lead me!

2015 Devotional Reading

I READ IN my devotional today:

> *When you are with other people, you often lose sight of My Presence. Your fear of displeasing people puts you in bondage to them, and they become your primary focus. When you realize this has happened, whisper My Name; this tiny act of trust brings Me to the forefront of your consciousness, where I belong. As you bask in the blessing of My nearness, My life can flow through you to others. This is abundant life!*

I have always wanted to please others. I never could. Or at least that is how I feel. I try too hard or not hard enough or I say too much or I don't say enough. I usually end up drowning in emotions and running! I usually end up running straight into a wall!

Communicating, talking, sharing is a learned trait. As children we quickly learn how our feelings are responded to. If we are feeling unloved or ignored, we make more noise. If that doesn't work we try different tactics: pouting, screaming, etc. If none of these tactics work we run and we pretend that we don't need attention or affection or love.

But communicating, really talking, really sharing is a not something I was taught and so many times I suck at it! I don't mean to. I don't want to. This ability of identifying feelings and where they come from and how I can respond to them is all in my growing process. It is in everyone's growing process. Some just get there faster than others and some never get there because they never try.

So here I am. I try and fall and try and fall and pick myself up and try and fall and on and on.......but I can't give up. I can't. I brush my knees off; I pick up the pieces of my broken heart and try to place it back in order. I don't want to stop trying. I don't want to stop growing. I read my Bible more, I pray more, and I talk to God. We seem to have developed this wonderful love relationship where I can go and ask, "God, am I doing okay? Help me, because I feel so alone in this journey." He squeezes my hand a little tighter to remind me that He is forever there and like it says in Psalms 23:5:

> *He anoints my head with soothing oil and my cup of cool refreshing love does runneth over and soon the table is set and I am sitting before my enemies and I have peace.*

Today I might not get it all right. I might not be able to communicate to others how I feel. You won't know what I so want to express. It might come out all wrong or maybe today, today I will get it right! Maybe today you will see kindness when you look into my eyes and genuine repentance. Either way, up or down, right or wrong whatever you judge, I want you to know in my heart I do try and I do repent and I do pray and I do, oh I do so want to get it right and I so want to love and be loved. And I do always find it in the arms of my Savior. That is where my peace comes from, my strength, my hope. That is where I grow.

I want to wear a T-shirt that says "I am not perfect, but love me anyway"

I want to scream, "Please don't expect me to always get it right. Please don't expect perfection from me." Clearly it says no one is perfect, no not one!

I don't want my relationship with anyone to be based on my performance. I won't ask that of anyone either. I promise you that I am trying and that I will always try to be the kind of person God wants me to be. But I can't live up to man's expectations. I can't live up to man's judgment. I won't perform ever again for love. I will genuinely try to do right and good by you because I love you, but not to gain your love.

I am different. Not worse, not better, just not you. Sometimes differences crash. Sometimes they crash hard! But that is only when they are running at each other full force. Otherwise they can learn to move together, they can learn to dance to each other's soul. I think I am tired of running full force into another's being, trying to get my voice heard, only to have created a crash so ugly. I think I am tired of running from another's being only to have them up to me and hit me hard while my back is turned. Yes, I am tired of it. Today I will dance. I will dance toward and around and over and through and under all the judgments, the anger, the differences and I will feel your pain too and your needs and I will let some of it attach to me, but only what I need to grow and learn from. I will move gracefully through and embrace the journey.

Because of heartache, pain, suffering, fear, whatever, we can succumb to a broken life. We can live in fear, in brokenness and we can slowly die inside, or we can fall at the feet of Jesus and allow him to work in our lives. Allow him to love us through the hell of earth. Allow God to love us. Accepting God's love is not always easy for some victims of abuse. It means that you are loved, and trusting that God knows what is best for us. Accepting unconditional love and trusting is very foreign to us. We must continue to walk in that love and trust and continue to believe.

Laura Kagawa-Burke

REFLECTION

The tragedy of life is not death. But what we let die inside of us while we live. Norman Cousins

This is exactly how I feel. My life is motion, one dance after another and with each new dance I am learning the steps. As I dance, as I sit in my art store I find my passions for what I love to do growing and becoming more aligned with my skills.

If we don't seek healing how can we receive it? The same is true with love. So many ways in my life journey hope could have died, love could have died or faith could have died. We must seek love in spite of the storms. Then we can help others as they make their way through the storms.

We must have faith. As my daughter explained and inspired me when she said, "Mom, anyone can pray for rain during a drought. Faith is holding an umbrella while you pray!"

Danielle, Fair Maiden

There is a beautiful maiden that lives by the sea
She writes beautiful words of sentiment that set my spirit free
All of her words have the magic that gives me life
Drinking in her wisdom that melts away my strife
For even in her youth, her soul is very wise
Her words bring forth the living, instead of dark demise
Beauty becomes her, for her heart is so pure
Her smile and gentle laughter seem to be a cure
This beautiful maiden, a poet is she
For when she writes her words of life, evil seems to flee
Strong words, life words. Words of love and pain
Words that are giving and seem to ease all pain
Fair is the maiden. This poet by the sea
Great is the love she gives so unconditionally to me
Where would I be without her words that make me dance?
I'd be lost without her poetry, stuck in circumstance.

VICKI WATKINS 2015

2015 Jim

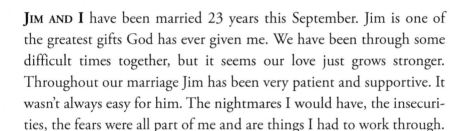

JIM AND I have been married 23 years this September. Jim is one of the greatest gifts God has ever given me. We have been through some difficult times together, but it seems our love just grows stronger. Throughout our marriage Jim has been very patient and supportive. It wasn't always easy for him. The nightmares I would have, the insecurities, the fears were all part of me and are things I had to work through. I still work on issues I have as a result of my past.

I won't say anymore. I have come to the place where I can love and forgive those who have hurt me. Some stay stuck. I could never have faked the medical experts, Jim or friends the terrible condition I have suffered or the results of my illness. I didn't ask for pity and I don't ask for it now. Not for anything I have ever been through or for anything I will ever go through. No, I don't want your pity or your hand out, but I will gladly admit I could use your love, your compassion, your encouragement, your friendship and I believe we all want and need those things from others. I want to love like God does. I want to give my best.

REFLECTION
Sometimes my feelings or emotions are very evident in writing this book. There were times in writing this book I wanted to quit, many times! But I am telling my story this once and I want the focus to be

on healing, on God's love and the hope He gives each of us. I am not living in the past. I live for the hope and the promises that today and tomorrow hold.

2015 Abe

SANDY MY COUNSELOR once told me that people treat us the way we allow them to treat us. She wasn't talking about abuse. When you are a child and someone abuses you, it is not your fault. When you grow up and seek healing and recovery you have to relearn many things. You have to learn what healthy relationships are and what are not. You learn to set boundaries, how to love someone and have boundaries. You grow and learn and grow and learn and you gradually begin to develop healthy relationships. You learn that just because you love someone that doesn't mean you have to accept disrespect. As we give it to others, we also learn to expect it from others. It becomes a natural healthy part of a relationship.

This has taken a lot of time for me: Learning how to love others in a healthy way, God's way. It has not always been easy for me. Often times I wanted love so bad that I allowed disrespect and abuse and denied my own needs or feelings. I either didn't think I deserved better treatment or really didn't know relationships were supposed to be better, probably both.

I am still working hard on this. For a long time I wanted my family's love so badly that I allowed them to call me names. I allowed them to disrespect me. I allowed them to walk on me. This doesn't mean I am responsible for their behavior. It just means that I accepted their behavior at a great cost to my well-being, to myself. I am not responsible for how they treat or speak to me, but I am responsible for accepting it and believing it. I am talking now as an adult that is growing and healing.

There comes a time when you realize you can't change others. You can't make them even feel the way you long for them to feel. You can't make them love you or respect you or encourage you or anything your heart might desire from them. You can only love them the way you want to be loved and step back and say what you did or what you said to me is not acceptable and I won't be in a relationship with you if this is how you treat me. It may hurt like hell to set that boundary at first, but in the long run it is very good for you. You are learning to give yourself the love and respect you lost and you are learning that you deserve that.

My growing phases have not always been easy for those people closest to me. I had to learn a balance. Having healthy relationships takes practice, especially for someone with my background. With my kids and with my husband I had to learn that screaming, fighting, trying to force my feelings on them did not make them understand me any better. It probably only made them want to scream back! When I learned to talk, to say that something hurt my feelings and here is why it did, they began to understand better. They also learn to talk to me when I in turn act or say something that hurts their feelings.

For example today I learned that my son Abe and Amy had a baby shower yesterday. (They are expecting their first child in September) Amy's mother gave them the shower. I was not invited. For whatever reason, maybe because we live in another state, they didn't include me. My feelings were very hurt. I could have responded in anger. I could have screamed and yelled. Instead I waited and prayed and then called them. I ask about the nice things they had gotten at the shower. I ask if they have everything they need now. I ask Amy how she was feeling. I waited and spoke in love. Then I said that I wish I had known about it. That my daughter Danielle and I would have flown in for their shower. I calmly said, "I want to be a part of your life events."

At first they were defensive and responded in trying to justify why I wasn't even invited. It was very hard for me not to respond hatefully. But I really am trying to do better, be better. So I simply said, I am not mad, I am not angry, I do not want to fight. I am simply saying my feelings are hurt that I wasn't invited.

I am leaving it there. I did cry when I got off the phone and I did tell God I was hurt and angry. I did talk to God about the emotions and feelings I was having. I was able to identify that I felt rejected. I have been rejected my whole life growing up so I hate that feeling! I really struggle with that emotion. But by identifying the emotion, by walking through it with God's help, I managed to not argue or fight. They didn't intentionally mean to hurt me, but it did hurt. And by talking about it respectfully I let them know that I was hurt and that I wanted to be included in their important events. I can only pray that it gets better in the future. I respected myself enough to say I really don't want to be treated this way; I want our relationship to be better.

This was a big step for me. I took care of myself. I had to then give it to God. I didn't want to make them feel bad. But I do want us to be considerate of each other's feelings and have respect for each other. Did I handle this perfectly? No, I will never, ever be anywhere near perfect, but I did handle it better than maybe I would have yesterday. I am learning. I am growing. I am enjoying this life God has given me.

2015 September

The Lord is my shepherd; I shall not be in want. He MAKES me lie down in green pastures, He leads me beside quiet waters, He restores my soul. He guides me in paths of righteousness for his name's sake. PSALM 23:1-3

SEPTEMBER HAS NOT been a good month for me health wise. I had vertigo attacks almost every day of the month. October started out the same. I also slipped and pulled my back out and it has been so painful. The pain goes all the way down my leg, waking me up at night. I resent my illness, I resent going to the doctor all the time, I resent, I resent, I RESENT! I could make a list of all the terrible unfair things that has happen to me. While reading this book, you might have thought "poor girl" or "how sad".

But I do have one choice, I can choose to feed the anger, the pain, the resentment or I can praise God for every breathe I take and every moment of living in His companionship, I will be honest, some days I don't do too good at letting go of all that ugly stuff. I stew a little, I pout some, I cry real tears and I feed the hurt and resentment.

Those are the days I really should release it all and place it at the feet of Jesus. Those are the days when I must force myself to count my blessings, dive into the word, cry in the arms of Jesus. But what if I am just too weary and I don't have the energy to go to God?

Psalm 23 says He makes me lie down in green pastures. God is a great Father. He knows when life gets too much. He knows our pain and like a good Father he says, "my child come, it's time to rest, give it all to me, you just lay here in beautiful green pastures. His word says, He MAKES me lie down in green pastures. God is not going to leave His child drowning in hopelessness. If He has to He will pick you up and carry you to those green pastures and lay you down to rest. Rest until our strength can be restored. Just cry out to him.

The doctor increased my medication, just for a while until my attacks calm down. My back will heal. Circumstances are constantly changing, life is a struggle at times, but there is also great joy.

Sometimes I have to stop, and lie down in green pastures of peace. Just lie there, searching for the joy of being in the Lord's presence. Searching for it like it is hidden treasure and it comes, it always comes.

Today I am weary. Take me to your green pastures Lord. Make me lie down, restore my soul.

2015 Vertigo Attack

CAN YOU READ what I have written on the next two pages? Try if you want and then read the poem below. This is how my attacks leave me.

Dear Friend,
I want to play but I can't, not today It's this silly head of mine,
Spinning around and around.
There is nothing I can do but wait it out And lay here.
Jesus sits here quietly, holding my hand. And I know I am not alone.
I whisper to him
"But Father I want to pray" And he promises me "Soon, Child, soon."
And I lay here with my eyes closed, writing This waiting for my head to get better.
I'm sorry friend, I really wanted to play today But this silly head just doesn't cooperate.
That is what my inner child says, that is how I feel. I try to be brave. I don't want to cry.
So I will just squeeze Jesus hand a little tighter. Sorry dear friend tomorrow we will laugh and play. Tomorrow I will be stronger.
Tomorrow God promises a new day.

Dear friend

I want to play but I can't
not today.
It's this silly, afraid of mine.
Spinning around a
Ground. There is nothing
I can do, but wait
it out and lay here.

Jesus sits here quietly)

holding my hand
and I know I am
not alone. I whisper
to him, But Father I
Want to pray and He promises

me soon, child soon.
And I lay her
with my eyes
Closed, waiting

So I just squeeze
Jesus hand a lil
tighter. Sorry dear
friend. tomorrow we
will play. Hold on
Play. Tomorrow I
will be stronger
Tomorrow God
promises a new
day

Love,
Zyri + God

This waiting for my
head to get better. I'm
sorry friend, I really
wanted to play today
but this silly head
just doesn't cooperate.
That is what my inner child
says, that is how I feel.
I try to be brave. I
don't want today.

2015 Beth

To bestow on them a crown of beauty instead of ashes,
the oil of gladness instead of mourning, and a garment of
praise instead of a spirit of despair. Isaiah 61:3

I HAVEN'T WRITTEN a lot about Beth. To be honest I didn't want to, too touchy a subject, too painful even after all these years. I feel like I have so much to say, too much to say and talking about it would just be useless; useless because no words could ever suffice my feelings.

I felt like everything is better left unspoken or at maybe everything is easier left unspoken. But God wants us to be whole, to be complete in Him, which means stripping off every weight that hinders us. Hebrews 12:1

I have carried this weight for a long time. It is really heavy and I think it's time I set myself free of it. I think I will try. Here goes…

Two days ago my very first grandchild was born. Alex came into our life weighing 7lbs. 8oz. He, with that adorable smile and deep brown eyes, is surrounded by love and family. He with his tiny hands and sweet smile came into this world surrounded by family that loves him. He was immediately loved and cherished. He is my very first grandchild.

Someone mentioned to me that Alex wasn't my first grandchild, since Beth the daughter I adopted out has children.

That one little statement packed a punch right to my gut! I don't want to talk about this; I don't want to address this subject. The hurt is still raw, still deep, buried like a deep seeded root, choking the promise of forgiveness. I can fake letting go, I can fake the smile, I can fake that I feel nothing, but in my body, in my soul I know.....I cannot not deny this root of pain, bitterness, anger, loss. I have done my share of root pulling in my time, worked on all the issues, studied all the statistics, fought so many battles, but only here, only for this brief moment will I admit that there still lives a deep seeded root of anguish inside of me and I pray that I have the strength and courage to get rid of it once and for all.

What does the Bible say about roots?

> *See to it that no one misses the grace of God and that*
> *no bitter root grows up to cause trouble and defile many*
> Hebrews 12:15

The grace of God is the only thing powerful to kill the root of bitterness. No bitter root should be allowed to take form, to grow, which I am pretty sure means, me running from this subject is not going to make it go away and it's never going to get rid of those ugly roots. I have been running from this subject all my life. I have never allowed anyone inside this subject, but today I am exposing it all. It is like I must stand naked before you and let go of all my shame.

Can I face this, my mind says no, my heart says no, my whole being screams no, but God says yes! God says

> *I can do all things through Christ which strengthens me.*
> Philippians 4:13

I gave birth to Beth. I loved her when I carried her in my womb and I loved her when I let her go. The circumstances of my pregnancy were not good. When I was younger, when I was stuck in the mire of hatred and pain I may have seen Beth as a consequence to awful sin. I may have look upon my pregnancy as a consequence to an offense played out against me. But the truth is Beth is not a consequence. She is beauty and life and love and goodness. She is laughter and smiles. She is strong and vibrant and caring and humble. She is created by the Most High God.

She is the perfect example of God's grace and she is not my daughter. Now hold on before you throw this book down! Hold on before you accuse me of being cold and rude. Let me explain that statement.

I am Beth's birth mother. I love her. It is that simple and yet that complex. I was not her mother when she was sick and needed care. I was not her mother when she fell and needed mommy kisses and a bandage. I didn't pray with her when she was growing up. I didn't see her walk her first steps or ride her first bike. I wasn't her mother. Her adopted mother was and is her mother. And although I loved her and I always will, I cannot carry the title of mother.

Beth and I mostly keep in touch on Facebook; occasionally a letter and pictures. I have never met Beth's children although their pictures are on my fridge. And I have never been their grandmother. I never played games with them or told them stories or held them or comforted them. I love them, I do. But I released my rights as mother and grandmother long ago. It was the most gut wrenching pain I have ever experienced and yet in the pain of it all, God brought forth Beth.

In Isaiah 61:3 it says that God gave them beauty for ashes. Beth is the beauty.

I love Beth, her husband and two children and that is both simple and complex. Simple in that nothing can change my love for her. Complex in that I don't really know my place in her life. Maybe I make it complex. Maybe my pain will always be raw and I just can't understand it all. Maybe some things are just too painful to keep revisiting. Maybe that makes me weak or selfish or all the above.

Today I am Beth's friend. I hope she understands what I have said at least a little bit.

So my biography reads like this, Abe is my oldest child. His son Alex is my first grandchild. Beth is a beautiful person, created by God's love in the midst of a tragic situation. Beth is the true reflection of God's hope. Beth's children are the offspring of all that is good. I am blessed enough to be their friend and to have the good fortune to love them. I can't go back and undo any of the things that have happened. I can only go forward. I can live in the abundance of God's Grace and Love. I can share that abundance to the best of my ability.

2015 Beth Visit

TODAY I WAS sitting in my store pricing items and I got a wonderful surprise! In walked Beth. It has been 17 years since I have seen her. We talk on Facebook and emails and such, but it had been that long since I had seen her.

She had flown into Cincinnati because her biological father's sister had passed away unexpectedly. She is only staying two days, but wanted to stop by and say hi. It was good seeing her. She is a very beautiful and caring person. She wanted to meet Danielle and she got to meet her, after Danielle got out of school. They had a nice visit.

She couldn't stay long because she had to go and be with her biological father's family. She left. I closed up the store and Danielle left to go home and I was to follow in my car. I cried all the way home. I screamed a little too. Oh and yes, I asked God, "Why?" I pulled over and had a really good cry.

Here are some of the feelings I had and I know that most of you won't understand them, or maybe the ones I want to understand them won't. I'll list the negative feelings first. I was feeling anger and fear and hatred and helpless and physically sick. I was so damn angry at God, my mom, my dad, Ted and mostly myself. Why God? I just want to know why you allowed Ted to enter into my life. Why didn't you stop him? Why me?

Melissa Hannon

LOVING ME

How many times do we all ask the WHY question when we are hurting? A million times? Why did this happen? Why? Why? Why?

And it seems at the time that God refuses to answer. I mean I sat there and waited for the big booming voice of God to answer me. If He would simply give me an answer then everything would be okay. Or would it? If I knew the answer, if you knew the answer to your why question, would it take the pain away? If you ask why did my spouse die or why did my child die or why was I abused or why did some guy lay on top of me and use me? If God answered us, would it take the pain away? Make it hurt any less? I don't think so. Deep gut wrenching pain sucks and nothing can ease that pain.

I asked God a lot of why questions while I sat in that car. Why did you allow it to happen, God? Why didn't you stop it? Why did you give me Lil and Ed for parents? Why was my dad an abusive drunk? I didn't hear any answer. I sat in my frustration for a few minutes. Although I tried hard to pout and not speak to God anymore the truth is, God sat with me, patiently waiting for me to calm down. I felt His love and I knew that I was alive and living and that I was so blessed. A wonderful husband, wonderful kids, wonderful grandson, a wonderful store, I could count my blessings all night. The why question had no answer that could possibly take the hurt away, it served no purpose.

So then I decided to let God know that I hated Ted! Hated my dad! Hated my mom! Hated myself! Wait a minute why did I hate myself? Oh there it was, the shame; the filthy shame that was like a black cloud that hovered over me and there was no escaping it. I was awful, I was dirty, and I was so ashamed! The truth was I hated myself more than any hatred I could conjure up to hate anyone else.

Then came the helpless feeling. I felt helpless. Beth was here, she was with him, her biological father and his family and I didn't want them anywhere near me. They had dropped her off to visit and pick her back up. Just outside. Just outside!

Now I could feel myself getting nauseated! I was sick to my stomach and I was sitting in my car acting like a fool or a wounded child. But wait I'm not a wounded, helpless child anymore. I have power and I can take control of all those feelings and give them all to God. Here God, you take them, they are way too powerful for me, but not for you. You can squash them like a bug!

So I prayed and I cried soft tears and I thanked God that I got to see Beth and that I love her and she loves me. I thank him for her life and I thanked Him that I was safe.

Now you might be asking why I had such a reaction. I should be thankful that I got to see Beth and I promise you I am. I do love her. I do want all that is good for her. I do want to be in her life. But I cannot stand the thought of him being in her life; him, her biological father. I know; I know God loves Him and maybe he is different. I thought I forgave him, I honestly wanted to but, maybe the best I can do is to wish him no harm or not to have a totally sucky life! Okay, that might not be forgiveness, I pray about it, I don't want bitterness, I just don't want to ever hear about him again and Beth is in his life. I understand her need, now I can only hope those who love me understand my need not to ever be reminded that he even lives.

There are going to be two sides to this argument - their side and mine. They will say he did nothing wrong. They will say he loved me. I am sure he told them that.

My side will say a 13 year old is a child. That was how old I was when we met. He shouldn't have been allowed to live with us. I shouldn't have been allowed to "date" a grown man at 13. And I use that word date loosely. I am diving in now; I am going to do this. This is the truth. I don't want to go there but, I have to, for the sake of healing and for the sake of all the young girls out there.

An adult man came into a 13 year old girl's life. He told her he loved her. He moved in. He lived in the same house with her. He told her that having sex was what people do when they love each other. He enjoyed himself.

I would lie in my bed at night, he in the room next to mine. I would drift off to sleep only to be awakened by him sneaking into my room. My doorway had beads that hung down and made noise when you walked through them. My mom's room was right across the hall from me. He would wake me up and take my underpants down and lay on top of me until he was done. I laid there. Wanting it to be over. There was no pleasure for me. No orgasms for me. I was sleepy and tired and I just wanted him to hurry and get done. There was no love making. No foreplay, not two lovers passionately making love. It was an adult man having sex with a young girl. It was all about him; all about his needs. I asked him several times if we could stop and wait until we got married. (He always told me he was going to marry me someday). But no, he said it was like we were married. One time after he had finished, we both fell asleep afterward. Mom caught him in my bed the next morning; him in his underwear. When she asked me, he said, "Don't tell her, they will make me leave." I did not enjoy the sex, but if this man left who would love me? That is what I felt at the time. So I lied to my mom about the abuse. Afterwards I again begged him to stop. Didn't I love him, he would ask. This is an expression of love. One time Ted borrowed his friend's apartment and we had sex there. He had just finished up when his friend came back. His friend knew what was going on. He called my mom. He told her what Ted was doing to me. He begged her to get Ted away from me. My mom got off the phone, told me what he said and ask me if Ted was having sex with me. "No,"

I answered. She walked away! She knew! Many years later, she would say she trusted me, that it was my fault. Dear parents please don't trust your young daughters to live with a grown man! Please don't think trust has anything to do with it. Protect them! It is your obligation as a parent!

I cried often. I was so confused. I thought Ted loved me and I wanted to be loved, but I hated being bothered all the time. That was what it was for me. Just like when my dad bothered me!

So here I sit, trying to explain to whoever will read this the sickness, the ugliness, the horror of it all and feeling so ashamed.

Beth, I love you. You are created by God and you are truly a gift from God. But I just cannot reconcile the love I have for you with the hatred of the abuse or the statutory rape or the ugliness of what he did to me. I want to have a relationship with you, but it must forever be separate from him and his world. You can love him, I understand that you only know him now, but I must forever keep my wall up. It is the only way I feel safe. I know this is all hard for you to understand. Please forgive me if I am not explaining it clearly. Just understand that my husband I and my kids are not a subject to ever be discussed with him. Nothing about me.

I never want to hear his name. I love you Beth. They say there are two sides to every story. I guess that is true. I am not asking you to choose, I am just asking you to understand that I cannot be anywhere near him. EVER!

REFLECTION

Today, December 7, 2015, I had an appointment with Sandy my counselor. We talked about Beth. I shared with her Beth's surprised visit and the feelings that I experience.

It was a gut wrenching session. Boy did I cry!

Beth has a relationship with her biological father. I haven't told Beth the circumstances of her birth. I haven't shared my story. I think I have been trying to protect her.

I got this forgiving thing all messed up in my head. I am a Christian and when I forgive an offense against me, no matter how ugly, I am releasing it from myself and giving it all to God. I am setting myself free. If I don't forgive then I carry the weight of that person's offense on my shoulders forever. You have to let it go to heal. Now here is where the hard part comes in. In forgiving I have to work through the anger, the tears, the pain, the shame, the bitterness, the I-want-to-punch-their-freaking-lights-out feeling!

It doesn't mean I am a bad person or not a good Christian when I felt those emotions. Sometimes those emotions come back, they pay me a visit and I have to again go to God with all of it.

When Beth surprised me with a visit and told me that she was in town to be with her biological father and his family after his sister had died. But I didn't want to hear his name. I didn't want him or his family dropping her off to see me! I have to be totally separated from him and the mention of him. That is my boundary that I have to have. I am going to tell Beth about John and I writing this book. I am going to ask her if she wants to read the draft. I am going to tell her that I cannot talk about the things that I have written. That if she wants to know the truth then she can read it.

Only with Sandy and Jim have I ever felt safe enough to speak these events out loud. That is why I had to email John back and forth in writing this book. I know it might be that old friend of mine "Mr. Shame" paying a visit. I don't know, but in reading this book, well maybe Beth will understand the walls I have had and the walls I am working so hard in knocking down. But boy does all of this knocking down of walls (healing) hurt like hell sometimes.

I was doing my Bible study this morning and came across just what I needed to hear after yesterday. In the First chapter of Ephesians this is how to change your identity: we are equipped through Christ with "every spiritual blessing" (v.3) chosen in Him "before the foundation of the world" (v. 4) regarded as "holy and blameless before Him" (v. 4) adopted through the "kind intention of His will" (v. 5) redeemed and forgiven, "lavished" with grace (v. 7-8) recipients of a glorious "inheritance" in heaven (v. 11) secured forever by "the Holy Spirit of promise" (v. 13-14)

2015 Uncle Brian

THERE ARE A few times in life when you meet that someone who touches your life in a very special way: Their thoughtfulness, their unconditional love, their attempts at always making peace, their wisdom and honesty and their willingness to accept you, for who you are and where you are at that moment. Their genuine care and concern for what you may be going through in life. Jim's Uncle Brian was one of those people.

Uncle Brian passed away a few days ago and this week is his memorial service. We cannot be at the service that is in Pennsylvania. But I wanted his family, his loving wife Cathy and sons Dan and Jeremy and daughter-in-law Abbey to know how very much we loved him and what he meant to us. We will forever carry his love and kindness in our heart.

We cry our tears for the loss of such a loving man and for all of you who must attempt to say good bye until we all join him again in Heaven. Although our arms are not physically around you, we embrace you with love and prayers and LOVE and more prayers.

Family is such a precious gift from God, it is to be cherished and loved and supported and accepted and for those who never get that or who never realized the significance of family, or the act of love and forgiveness, they are forever wandering in a cold world never finding the warmth of love and grace.

Uncle Brian you were always so very kind to Jim and I. We will forever love you and forever hold you in our heart. Our gift to you now is to always love Aunt Cathy, Dan, Jeremy, Abbey, Grant and their baby-to-come and to stay in close contact and to cherish every moment that we walk this earth together.

PART THREE

Laura Kagawa- Burke

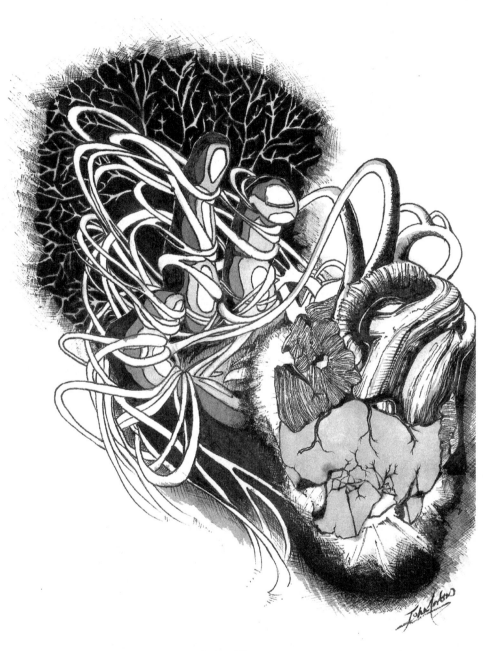

John Martino

MY HEART

If my heart could speak what would it say
Would there be too many broken pieces that would get in the way

Would the puzzle piece together with a bold message to read
Would the message be of love or of a violent deed

Would hope seep out with joyful tears
Or would it be too dark, shadowed by my fears

If my heart was free to speak to you
Would it speak compassion or bitterness blue

If suddenly my heart was free and you could place it in your hands
Would it crumble when you held it or boldly take a stand

Would it pulsate rapidly, forgiveness and love
Or would it forever rest, destroyed by what wasn't spoken of

If my heart could speak, if my heart was free
If you had to face the heart of me

Would you run or in your ego take a stand
Would you listen, would you love it as you held it in your hand

Could you accept the broken pieces that you shattered along the way
Or would you drop it, in fear of what it might say

If my heart could face you, if you could hold it in your hands
If it could give you a message, make you understand

I think it would simply beat, strong and loud
I think it would love you, forgive and be proud

For you would simply have no power, you would lose that today
For I am loved by God and that is all it has to say

VICKI WATKINS 2015

Sydney Burris

2015 Home

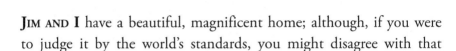

JIM AND I have a beautiful, magnificent home; although, if you were to judge it by the world's standards, you might disagree with that statement.

It is a very small three bedroom, one bathroom ranch house on a crawl space. It doesn't have a basement. It needs some repairs. The gate on our fence falls off the hinges if you aren't careful and we could use some new windows and gutters. Our bathroom is small and needs updated. But…to me it is absolutely beautiful!

To me it is home… my first real home!

I have lived many other places, but I never had a home before this one. I feel love there. I have cried there and laughed there and always felt safe there. I have decorated it on tiny budgets and played games with the kids there. I have eaten popcorn and watched movies with my husband there. I have read some really good books there and turned up my stereo there. I have danced around the rooms there, being silly with my daughter. I have curled up on my bed and felt rest there. I have grieved for those I lost there. I have gotten aggravated because we didn't have the money to repair things there. I have been seriously sick there. And I have ALWAYS felt safe there!

Jim and I bought the house in 1996, our first home, our forever home. Jim and I have had a lot of obstacles to go through in our marriage. Nasty custody battles for the boys, expensive legal fees, my brain tumor surgery, my illness, co-pays for doctor visits, and balances from what insurance wouldn't pay for procedures, surgeries and tests. We never moved up into a bigger house because we live within our budget. We couldn't afford a bigger house with a bigger house payment. So the years flew by. And the memories grew with each passing day. And a house became a home and beauty seeped through the small cracks and for the little girl in me it became HOME and I love it! And there is love there. And as I keep repeating… I feel safe there.

REFLECTION

Funny how we can take so many things in life for granted. We don't necessary mean to, we just do. Because of my history, because of what I lacked growing up, materially or emotionally, I find it easier to be really grateful now. I write in my blessing book all the time. Listing the many blessings God has given me. Thanking God. Thank you for everything, Dear God.

I thank God for our house, for our home. For our cars, for our food, for His provision, for His love, for my husband, kids, the list goes on and on. Think about all the blessings in your life.

2015 Closure

DO YOU KNOW how many hurting people there are in the world? Far too many to count! How about in your state? Your city? Still far too many to count! How about on your street?

John, both of us know the hole that is left in the heart of someone broken. Whether it is the painful loss of a child or the horror of abuse or the battle of an illness, how we stagger through the storm, how we survive is important. We all know we will be forever changed, but changed is so much better than destroyed! You and I were not destroyed! Bent but not broken… although there were times when I am sure we both felt like we were in a million pieces. But we had hope…people need hope.

Hope comes from our Heavenly Father. He gives us hope. It is there for everybody in every storm. We just have to help others find it… find Him. Because not only does hope come from the Father… hope is the Father. Our book is a small instrument of that hope!

> *I believe closure is possible, but it does not come the way people expect or want. The closure comes from within, by completing the grieving process, by accepting that the perpetrator and probably the court system and other various entities are not going to 'get it' the way the victim desires. Closure comes in being restored to authentic*

identity and prospering in life and relationships even though the perpetrator does not take responsibility or gets to hear from the victim.

Rachel Davis, MS, CFLE, Co-Founder Connections: A Safe Place

I cannot speak for others. I can only speak for myself. Many people have often told me to move on, let go and forget the past. While I wish that total forgetfulness was possible, it is not. But I have learned that there is healing and new life and I believe all of that begins with Jesus. His word says he makes all things new.

As far as closure is concerned I feel that in my heart I have found it. If given the chance I wouldn't want to confront my parents or anyone who has ever hurt me. One day in therapy Sandy explained it to me just this way in a parable. She asked me to imagine that my father had died and was sitting in a big room. All around him were filing cabinets. The whole room was full of them. Dad sat there in this room all alone. He waited and waited for someone to come. Growing restless he started looking in the filing cabinets. There was file after file of terrible things a man had done: abusing his wife, his children, neglect, violence, and drinking; one terrible file after file. Dad kept reading. "This man is awful." he thought.

Finally Jesus entered the room. My dad told Jesus about the files he had been reading. This man is awful; he has done some awful things. Who is he? "You," Jesus answered. Dad got up and ran to the file cabinets. He started pulling out drawer after drawer, file after file. All the sins had been erased. All the files were empty. That is what God's love is. That is what His love does for us.

Allison Hess

After I was told that story, I thought about all the times I hurt someone, the tears I caused, the sins I did. I can't imagine how awful I would feel sitting in that same room only the files would have my sins on them.

We all stand before God when we die. Some people won't ever see their files wiped cleaned, others will. But for those moments when we stand before God, we will know that we too have caused someone pain.

LOVING ME

For me that is more than enough. All the anger and hate I have felt for those who hurt me can never be as awful or cause them as much grief as when they stand before the Lord with their shame. And they will feel shame because one cannot be in the presence of such love and holiness and not see and feel the contrast of darkness.

This book is not about revenge or hatred although many acts of revenge and hatred have been done. It is about how the sweet, pure love of Jesus makes all things new.

There is closure in the arms of my Savior.

2015 Maine Trip

JOURNAL ENTRY **8/10/15** Monday 4:16 pm

*We are in the car heading home. We will take our time and prob-
ably stop and spend the night half way. We are going home a different way than we came. We are going to go through Vermont and see
some covered bridges.*

*This vacation has been amazing! We visited Salem and Boston,
Mass. We visited Booth Bay, Maine and Cape Elizabeth. We went
sailing in Maine for 2 and a half hours and the ocean was so beautiful! We saw some seals. I can't begin to thank God enough for this
vacation and my husband Jim too. I have always wanted to go to
Maine. It was all I imagined and more.*

*This vacation was long coming for Jim and me. And it was much
needed. To be able to travel and take our time and see God's
creation and drink in His beauty, has been a very humbling
experience.*

*A lot of things have been long coming for me. Healing, hope,
peace, growth....the journey has been so very painful and difficult
at times. I was so timid and scared and weak and I fought and I
fought and I continue to grow and I continue to press on. I go back*

and reread my journals of long ago and it amazes me that I survived, that I not only survived but I grew, I healed, I fought and I still do.

I only had one attack while on vacation. It was a bad one, but it happened in our hotel room. I could take my meds, lie down and be still. It didn't happen on the beach, or in the tourist places we visited. It didn't happen on that beautiful sail boat ride. It didn't happen when I was sitting on the rocks watching the waves crash against them. I didn't want it to happen at all. I am tired of the attacks, but if it did have to happen, then I thank you God that it was there in the hotel room.

I have been thinking about circumstances. I have prayed a lot to you Lord over all these years. I have asked you to take away so many bad circumstances. I think I sat waiting for you to rescue me from all the pain and ugliness. I knew you would come, like a knight riding in on a white horse and you would slay the demons and hurt all those who hurt me. And they would feel my pain and they would regret ever hurting me. But you didn't come, dear God.......well not like that......not like I wanted you to come. You left me there in those furious flames of bitterness and abuse. You left me there and I felt so alone and so helpless. I loved you, even when you didn't rescue me. Just like your Son Jesus, when he asked you to take this cup from him.

You didn't take my cup from me, not literally removing it, but you did physically come and stand beside me and you felt my pain and my sorrows and my helplessness and fear, you felt every minute of it and you took that load with you to the cross. You felt everyone's pain and sorrow. You carried the weight of the world. I can't explain it, and to be honest there is this big part of me that would have loved to have been rescued, completely removed from the circumstances,

from the situations. But I know and no one can tell me any differ-
ently that the only way a person can survive in the worse of circum-
stances is to have your presence there. Now when I have my physical
setbacks, attacks, I pray God heal me, but if not then don't you dare
leave me! I can't walk this alone. Because now I know that it is only
in your presence that I can ever live.

Luke 8:43 tells the story of a woman who had an issue of bleeding
for 12 years. No one could heal her. A huge crowd of people crowded
around Him as he tried to walk through the town. The woman who
had an issue of bleeding knew that if she could just get close enough to
touch Jesus' cloak she would be healed. She pressed through the crowd
until she could touch the edge of His cloak.

This woman had an issue of bleeding. More than anything she wanted
to be healed. She wanted the pain, the discomfort, the stink of constant
bleeding to be gone. She pressed on until she could touch His cloak.

We all have issues. Some of us have more than others. Receiving healing from traumatic abuse is hard and painful. In can be a life time
of pressing on, pressing toward recovery, pressing and pressing and
pressing on, forward. In writing this book many, many times I wanted to quit. I wanted to turn away, it all seemed too much. But I press
on because I know what lies ahead: healing and wholeness, life and
acceptance.

For I know the plans God has for me. Jerimiah 29:11

There are those times when I get stuck. When I can't seem to take
another step I surround myself with good resources - people who love
and build me up, people who encourage me to press onward. I have
had and still have professional counselors and resources in my life that
encourage me to press on. I study God's word; I drink in God's truth. I

admit when I get stuck and I ask for help. I then get back to the place where I can press on.

There were many times in my life that I felt alone, when I didn't have the resources or know of the people that could encourage and help me to press on. That is when God intervenes - Paula my best friend who invited me to Sunday School, a teacher, Ann, Dr. Hanson, Dr. Sweeten's LifeWay, Sandy, Rachel & Rebecca, Connections support group, a helping hand, a warm and tight hug, a small glimmer of hope............

It is very important to be that hug, that hand, that hope in someone's life. No act of love is too small. Never think that because you can't do a lot or something big that you just won't do anything at all. Don't ever think that what you have to give is not important or big enough.

I had a lot of really bad, hurtful things done to me, but I have had a lot of really great things done for me. No matter if your day is sunny or you are weathering the worst storm ever........ You are loved and you are never alone.

I will never leave you nor forsake you. Joshua 1:5

It might feel like you are forsaken, but don't trust that feeling; it is just stinking thinking. Trust the evidence of the sunshine in your life before, during and after every storm. The "son" doesn't disappear during storms; you just have to look behind the clouds. I seek God and find Him everywhere. His love is evident in creation, in laughter, in children at play, in wisdom of the elderly, in the eyes of friendship, in a helping hand, in my hope,

2015 Under the Stars

I AM SITTING at my desk in the art our gallery "Under the Stars" that I own. It is a beautiful day in late August. We aren't having the usual summer heat; it feels more like a cool autumn day. I look around at all the beautiful art that surrounds me, creating by very talented artists from all over the U.S. I feel so alive. I love how the art makes me feel and the wonder of it. I am amazed at the talent that God has given these artists.

To the right of my desk is a sign that a friend gave me that reads "It is Well with My Soul." I love that sign. As I sit here, I know I can feel it; it is well with my soul! I never thought I would be able to say that or feel that.

Today I am able to sit at my computer and write. I am able to have my own business and I am able to say that I have had my book of poetry published and that I am happily married and that my kids have grown up to be amazing adults. I have a deep soul abiding relationship with my Savior and Lord and I have an abundance of loving friends. I am safe and my health has improved so much. Yes, today It Is Well With My Soul and I am so very, very thankful.

Today I try so hard not to take any moment, anything for granted. I live in each moment and experience love and laughter much more that pain and bitterness. I forgive those who have hurt me and love them in a safe way. I believe in the impossible and seek out the miracles of God. I giggle more than I ever had and I love to play! Play barefoot in the grass or my toes in the sand. I love to call my friends just to say hi and send out cards and greetings for no real reason other than love. I love to flirt with my husband and hold his hand. I delight in my relationship with my Lord and my grown kids. I love to look at the stars and watch lightning bugs and full moons. Sandy beaches and the vast oceans make me want to dance with delight! I love the mysteries of life and creation. Chewy chocolate and a good book are favorites I treasure. Giving love and receiving love are some of the very best. Yes, today I live in life! I drink it in and every moment becomes a part of me and it is well........

But yesterday, well yesterday there was a broken little girl, a frightened and wounded inner child, a hopeless, reckless adult person wandering in what seemed like a forever lost world. Yesterday, I cried a million tears, I fought a million battles, I battle demons and darkness, I cowered in fear and I persevered in God's strength. Yesterday I thought all hope was lost and there was moments that I was certain they would be my last. Deep in my soul there will always be a small speck of yesterday and that is okay, because yesterday has no power over me anymore. I can live with that speck of yesterday because today is so much better.

2015 Alex

JOURNAL ENTRY - September 30, 2015

> *Yesterday God blessed me with a beautiful grandson, my first grandchild. My son Abe and his wife Amy live in Texas, so Jim and I haven't got to meet him yet. We are flying down next week. His name is Alex and he is beautiful! In his pictures he favors both Abe and Amy. I have not held him and yet my heart is overflowing in love.*
>
> *My son has a son! I am a grandmother!*
>
>> *For you created my inmost being;*
>> *You knit me together in my mother's womb.*
>> *I praise you because I am*
>> *fearfully and wonderfully made;*
>> Psalm 139: 13 - 14

All of us are fearfully and wonderfully made; created by a loving God. How great is our Heavenly Father's love for us. If only we could remember the depth of his love every second of every day. I think it was like that in the beginning, in the Garden of Eden, before sin.

I cannot fathom how a parent can deliberately hurt their child. I know we as parents don't always get it right, but a deliberate abuse?

Brokenness, anger, hatred, violence........what has been given to us as we grow up in this world? What do we pass down to our children? Can we start fresh? Start new? Can we break the chains that bind? I believe we can. We start at the cross. We give it all to Jesus. We replace it with His love and forgiveness and tenderness.

So here's to you Alex. Beautiful tomorrows, endless laughter, warm hugs and chains forever broken.

Journal Entry - October 9, 2015

Today Jim, Danielle and I flew to Texas. Today I held our grandson Alex in my arms for the first time. He is 10 days old.

Big brown eyes looking at me. The moment I first held him, I fell in love. This tiny being looking at me. His tiny hand in mine. I spoke softly to him and whispered I love you in his tiny ear. Did he know? Could he feel the love overflowing from me to him?

My spirit was soaring. My soul took flight and everything that ever was and everything that will ever be was good and right and just. In that moment life didn't have to make sense, questions didn't have to be answered, all wrongs were made right and for that moment it was 100% well with my soul.

For in that moment in the innocence of a newborn, in a love so endearing it was well with my soul!

The past is gone, I have moved beyond the past. This book is my way of letting it go, releasing it. The future is in the hands of my Savior, with whom I trust. There is just this moment, this precious moment, where my grandson Alex lays in my arms and I look into his big brown eyes and whisper a prayer of thanks and blessings. Completely surrounded by God's love and presence.

And I know that God in His goodness has brought us together. Today, right now, IT IS WELL WITH MY SOUL!

REFLECTION

Our deepest fear is not that we are inadequate. Our deepest fear is that we are powerful beyond measure. It is our light, not our darkness, that most frightens us. We ask ourselves: Who am I to be brilliant, gorgeous, talented, and fabulous? Actually, who are you not to be? You are a child of God. You playing small does not serve the world. There is nothing enlightened about shrinking so that other people won't feel insecure around you. We are all meant to shine, as children do. We were born to make manifest the glory of God that is within us. It's not just in some of us; it's in everyone. And as we let our own light shine, we unconsciously give other people permission to do the same. As we are liberated from our own fear, our presence automatically liberates others.

Marianne Williamson *A Return to Love: Reflections on the Principles of a Course in Miracles*

2015 The Porch

THERE IS A front porch in the hills of Kentucky that I love to sit on. The front porch is attached to my cousins Linda and Eddie's house. They, along with their grown daughters and grandchildren have kind of adopted me. They love me, their love is unconditional. And I am crazy about all of them.

Love grows there in their house and laughter and kindness. Warmth and peace and smiles and giggles are alive on that front porch. On summer days when I visit, I will sit on their front porch and look out on their farm. I will feel the breeze on my face or watch a humming bird drink from a feeder. I will laugh at the stories I hear or engage in conversation about everything or nothingness.

They are cattle farmers. I will listen as they share their latest cattle adventure or show they had been too. I am a city girl born and raised and although the country life is in many ways foreign to me, I never feel like a foreigner there. My lack of knowledge and country living isn't evident as we all visit together on their front porch.

We are family there. Laughing, giggling, visiting. I am safe there and loved. They are really good people.

I would never want to live in the country. I have too much city in me, but I love visiting there. I love the peace I feel there and their love. God brought them into my life just a couple years ago. I didn't know them too well until then. But like all of God's gifts, getting to know them, falling in love with them came at the perfect time. Their love is a constant encouragement. Having their love in my heart often gave me the courage to continue with my story. I hope someday soon that Linda and Eddie will sit on their porch on a warm summer day, with a cool glass of tea and read this book. And I hope they know that they are a huge part of my wholeness and life.

This book is not the end of my story; it is just part of my story. The best is yet to come!

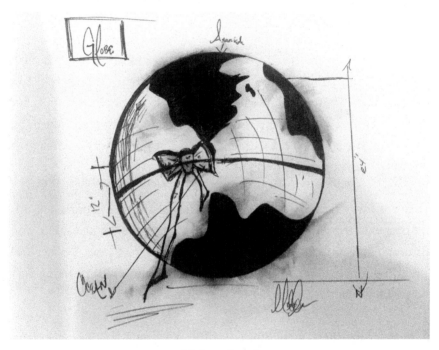

Melissa Burch

Blizzard Wishes

I wish for ribbon
And a lot of it
Enough to tie around the world and finish it off with a lopsided bow
Because that's the only bow I know how to make
And should I succeed in this decorative endeavor I would then wish
    for a mirror, the size of the sun,
So that I may show the world what I had done
And say to it "Here, you are
A little broken
And a little off
But add a little spirit
And you look mighty fine"
And that's fine, to only look fine once a year
And it's finest of all at this time of the year
When frost begins to form over windshields like diamonds encrusted
    over a Faberge egg impossibly delicate and incredibly fragile
Like dreams that melt away the moment you touch them with your
    reality-warmed hand
I never feel as in tuned to the world as I do when snowflakes fall one
    atop the other,
These miniscule pieces merge together to make for a school child's
    dream - a snow day
Even more extraordinary than that, the idea that when billions of
    these creations - each one no bigger than a centimeter - meet each
    other on the top of a thousand foot mountain they can make an
    avalanche
I wish the world would see what I see
The truth of it all
I wish the world would see what we are
We are snowflakes
Seven billion tiny, insignificant snowflakes

On a sphere shaped mountain
Spinning in a circle with more force than any dreidel ever made
We are the ice crystals dancing over the mountain's face
We are snowflakes
And like snowflakes, when we combine and move as one we can form
   avalanches
We can begin revolutions with nothing more than our bodies and our
   limbs which move us forward
Like glaciers we do not simply glide over land
But we carve into it,
We can mold the Earth with our own hands
Even more so when our hands are holding each other
Because a snowstorm is powerful thing
But do not underestimate a single snowflake
Which of us here has never been walking outside
From the car to our school or to our house or to a store and seen
A single snowflake
That spun in the air like a prima ballerina
Performing in her first ballet
In the school performance of
The Nutcracker
Who here, seeing that single snowflake,
Which danced before its brothers were ever born
Would not smile
And think
"What a pretty snowflake I wish that it were mine"
Or even perhaps
"What a pretty snowflake I wish that it were me"
What some of us would give to be allowed to dance on air,
Blown to and fro, but never falling victim to the wind
For no one is afraid of falling just of hitting ground
How strange it must be to be a snowflake
Existing both for the lack of heat and for the presence of water

And I wish I had a mirror
Big enough to show the world how at any given moment
The Earth is both enveloped by night
And illuminated by day
If only you could see that even in the coldest moments
There is still warmth
And even in the darkest night
There is still light
Whether it be the holy light of angels
Calling to sleeping shepherds
Saying "Come and see"
Or if lights are manmade glows in the form of LED
Or candles on menorahs
The porch light by the front door
Lighting your way home
Or the blue electric glow of your phone
At night
Texting your best friend
There is always light
I wish I could illuminate the world
Enough to show the tapestry loom
Wherein the patterns of life and death are interwoven in beautiful
     waves
Like the voices in a children's choir
Chaotic, mismatched and ill formed
But so beautiful
And the choir sings out
A plaintive song
Almost indiscernible over the noise of pipe bombs
And argumentative politicians
I wish I had a microphone loud enough to send the song
Out, ringing into the furthest reaches of the Milky Way, so that even
     the asteroids would note the chords of humanity's anthem

And I wish I could hire a thousand translators, one for each language,
	to convey to each country the lyrics to the lachrymatory
	lamentation that is -
Peace on Earth Goodwill to men -
Because what is this verse but a wish?
The ultimate wish
For light and kindness
In a world full of hatred and darkness
And there is no wish more pure than this-
And there is nothing I wish more than this
That there may -
Even if it lasts only a day -
Be peace at last
And if this wish is impossible
-As most beautiful things are -
And if it is impossible that for one day all men may throw down their
	weapons
Put aside their hate
Forget their thirst for vengeance
And see each other through eyes as pure as the driven snow.
Then allow me one last wish
I wish that you may be at peace
That your heart may be filled by the most pleasant light
And that that light may shine out of your skin like starlight seen
	through clouds
So that all that see you, see hope
Even if they don't recognize it at first
And if for religion or poverty you receive no gifts I wish to give what
	little gifts I can
I offer you comfort
- In the knowledge that though there is sometimes darkness, there is
	always light -
I offer you freedom

- In that even if your limbs are useless burdens your mind can wander
    freely -
I offer you love
- In the form of my own heart, which breaks to think you might feel
    broken -
I offer you my hand
- In that we may walk together through snow and brush -
I offer you shelter
- In my house you all are welcome to sit around the fire and let water
    fall from your eyes (tears or melting snow flakes, I won't ask) -
I offer you these gifts in the hopes that you may take one - or take all
    - and know that you are not alone
Lastly I offer you this I offer you a chance
Smaller than an ice crystal
And twice as fragile
More glorious than the northern lights
And as careful as a child
Who for the first time is allowed to participate
To hang up the glass balls
And shimmering garland
And grandma's angel atop the Christmas tree
May you be filled with more joy
Than when that same child is told
"Well done"
I offer you a wish
And I pray it may be granted.

Danielle Watkins 2015

Addendum

Your story could be the key

That unlocks someone else's prison.

Don't be afraid to share it!

PASTOR JOHN HAGEE

You will land on your feet
Just let go.

Glenn Martin Taylor

To Those

To those who tried to break me, you did not succeed
Although certainly you wounded and left me to bleed
God had other plans, as He touched each scar
The battle isn't over, not by far
The spirit of deceit you tried to send my way
Quickly tried to choke me and make me its prey
But there is a voice that is rising and it is so clear
The voice tells me not to run or give in to this fear
The spirit of infirmity was the next strategy you planned
 And although it tried to cripple me, here I still stand
So as you gather up your posse and treat me with contempt Surely I
    am weary, but I am not yet spent
The fingers that are pointing in their judgment and their pride Don't
    see the line is drawn now and I no longer hide
So to those who tried to break me in your constant pursuit
Know that I am anchored in a love that has forever taken root
A new dawn is breaking and with it comes God's peace
As all the forces of darkness fall and your hatred has to cease
To those who still want to break me, know it can't be done
 The battle is already over and you haven't won

Vicki Watkins 2015

Bill Dirkes

LOVING ME

On the Healing and Growth of Vicki Watkins – Gary Sweeten, D.Ed

When I read about Vicki's warm reception by Pam Hanson I wept. The power of caring in a usually cold and clinical medical office provided the foundation for so much growth and healing. The devastation of shame can be penetrated slightly and allow the truth of God's creation enter for a millisecond and provide the necessary hope for moving on to fight the lies of the enemy and overcome them more and more by renewing the mind.

The average time a Doctor listens to a Patient is 37 seconds! Pam and her Nurse embraced, listened and fed Vicki. What an amazingly powerful knock on the door of Vicki's heart by Jesus.

It is clinically relevant to the core ideas on which we established LifeWay. It is exactly how we attempted to walk out our ideas about a building a Therapeutic Community on a daily basis with fragile people like Vicki and Ann. The healing fellowship these two experienced before and after every clinical session was foundational to our theology and our psychological theory. I had written and taught about The Church as a Therapeutic Community for years and God gave us an opportunity to establish it at Emerson A. North Hospital.

The two essential dimensions of a Therapeutic Community are Communitas and Healing Charisma. Communitas is accepting people completely just as they are with no barriers to entry. Only persons who admit they are unworthy to earn entry can be admitted. Alcoholics are invited to attend AA if the admit they are drunks. People can be admitted to a church fellowship if they admit they are unchristian sinners.

Another part of Communitas indicates that although we accept sick people into the hospital we will do everything within our power to heal you. The unloving person will be loved into wholeness and the sinner will be loved into holiness. The tag line of "Come as you are, and you will be loved". It is not accepted and affirmed because that would encourage brokenness not health. It is therapeutic only if it is accepted and loved.

This is what Dr. Hansen did when she and her team accepted and loved Vicki just as she was. There were no barriers to her because she was a mess of emotions and behavior. They cared, nurtured and then referred her to LifeWay, another place where she could be accepted and counseled.

The meaning of Healing Charisma is also unique for it states that a community is most healing when the gifts, love and help come from the entire community. They do not rest exclusively in the Professionals or staff. Credentials are not necessary to be a source of Healing Charisma. LifeWay was intentionally designed to offer this second factor.

The approach at LifeWay was based on a 1975 dissertation for an E. D. in Counselor Education that led to the discovery of the Therapeutic Community movement championed by Dr. Maxwell Jones of England. It is based on basic Christian principles of equality and church community that we developed at College Hill Presbyterian Church, Social Learning Theory, and the idea that Psycho Education were the most powerful sources of healing and growth.

Most traditional in-patient units operated on the basis of a strict hierarchy with little input from Nurses, Counselors, and Social Workers. Patients and their families and supporters had no input into the assessment or treatment of the residents. We turned that idea around and invited anyone from the home base of the Patient to come to regular group sessions each week. We saw that how the individuals were treated upon return to real life was a key to ongoing health. Normal hospitals had little therapeutic group work each day.

A powerful way to build a Therapeutic Community is to involve the Residents in role plays and psychodrama where they actually develop the script and play various roles of past events to relive them in order to get a new perspective on painful times and share it in a safe environment.

This was especially powerful when family members came to sessions with Residents and other families. We taught each Resident the basic principles of Family Dynamics and each did a Genogram which could provide a great deal of data for healthy discussions. Those Genograms were often share and used as Psychodrama scenes at Family Nights.

LifeWay averaged eight hours each day in order to "Equip God's people to minister to each other. That way we mobilized the resources of each resident to offer care and encouragement to others." The Residents were fellowship so our staff trained them how to nurture and care for each other. The Apples of Gold classes taught listening with love as a foundation to all else and the Renewing the Mind classes taught everyone how to stop stinking thinking and adopt the mind of Christ. Pam Hanson had been trained in Apples and Rational and applied those skills with Vicki in her Medical office!

The Apples of Gold training was designed to equip every Physician, Counselor, Nurse and Social Worker the basic attitudes and skills that have been revealed by extensive research to be foundational to every person that wishes to foster healing and growth in other persons. In summary, the Core Conditions of Healing are: Genuineness, Respect, Empathy and Warmth.

Genuineness is the ability to relate to others in a natural, sincere manner rather than as a special person with credentials and position. Respect is treating others as equal in personhood. It is the belief that everyone, especially those bruised and broken by life, have the potential to grow in self-efficacy or self-choices. It rejects the idea that a Therapist can treat Clients as lower than they without harming them.

Empathy is the ability to understand another person's thoughts and feelings in such a way that the person believes he/she is being genuinely known. It is not feeling another person's feelings.

Warmth has to do with liking people in such a genuine manner that our non-verbal behavior shows it. It is communicated primarily through tone of voice, smiles, tears, posture, etc.

When a person has these characteristics those with whom they interact will generally grow emotionally, relationally and spiritually. It can be summarized by the tag line, "People do not care how much we know until they know how much we care." As a result we had summarized these skills into teaching manuals for our church called Apples of Gold after the scripture found in Proverbs 25:11. The main focus of our basic work can be found in the Bible passages that teach us about the Fruit of the Spirit. We trained hundreds of people in our and other congregations how to "Speak the truth in love" and we transferred that model into the LifeWay Unit and trained not only the staff but also the Residents.

Training Residents/Patients was and still is a unique approach rarely if ever replicated except by those few places that believe that the community itself is the most powerful source of growth and healing. This mirrors the notion that the key to health lies in Communitas and Healing Charisma, or as the Bible says, Mercy, Grace and Love with Truth.

In addition to learning how to relate with the Fruit of the Spirit, we added to the church curriculum and thereby to the hospital, God's Truth applied in a practical manner to the past, present and the future. We had seen this work miracles of change when we equipped hundreds of people in our church. They learned how to exchange the lies of the world for the truths of God. Lies end up as "Stinking Thinking" or self-talk filled with self-condemnation, self-hatred, anger, bitterness and chronic mood disorders of anxiety and depression.

Another course was Breaking Free From the Past which trained the Residents, who were 99% Christians, how to engage in Prayer Therapy, offer and receive forgiveness, etc. We used the 12 Steps of AA to guide our work.

One of the most powerful courses was How to be Me in My Family Tree which looks at receiving generational blessings and breaking generational curses. These also built on the Apples, RCT and Breaking Free Classes. (All these materials are available at www.sweetenlife.com)

Vicki was also involved deeply in the individual Counseling as well as the group classes and therapy so she learned how to give assistance as well as how to receive it from others. However, from reading her story it appears that she gained greatly from the living milieu by boarding with Ann, a lovely, motherly role model.

It is a common experience for deeply traumatized persons to continue to heal and grow for many years. Recovering from deep and continued trauma and abuse is like recovering from heart surgery. The abuse and toxic stress of being reared in a home where nurture was missing and adversity was daily leaves the heart and soul of a child in a terribly vulnerable and easily triggered. Like a bruise or internal damage from an accident, the emotional bruises of adversity can be hard to overcome.

There is a great deal of emphasis on the damage being done to children and youth by Adverse Childhood Events. There is even a new term being used to discuss it: Trauma Informed Therapy. Shock, Trauma and Abuse leave a trail of destruction to people reared in homes where positive behaviors are rare. Neglect and negative behaviors are common.

Intrusions: The lack of warm nurture and the presence of active intrusions each leave a child emotionally and physically damaged.

The brain does not develop properly and the part of the brain that absorbs emotional memories becomes intensely guarded and on high alert most of the time. It can leave a person desperately in need of nurture and care and vulnerable to the promises of love and acceptance by predators and manipulators.

Just as a child born with a heart valve defect may need surgeries and treatments at various stages of growth so does a child that suffers from an emotional heart defect. The healing/growth process may procced slowly and slowly throughout the early years even when the child is rescued from her toxic environment and placed into a loving, nurturing home in the case of some adoptions and foster care.

We developed LifeWay to start the healing process and teach our Residents how to apply the principles with the Psychoeducation classes. Secondly, we taught daily about the fact that sanctification or Christian growth is a lifelong process. We will never stop growing and we will never stop needing to be healed until we reach heaven. Unfortunately, bad theological ideas have convinced many that total healing and perfection is possible as the result of a dramatic spiritual experience. Nothing leads to more despair and loss of healing that this false hope because it rests on the self-effort of the believer rather than the finished work of Christ.

There are four main issues that beset all persons as a result of the fallen nature: Dead in Sin (Disease), Pride (Self Righteousness), True Guilt (Justice Deserved for Failures), and Loss of Identity (Not a child of God). When we come to faith in Christ we are:

Reborn from Death and Made alive in Christ.
Converted from Selfishness to Rest in Christ.

Justified and Forgiven from Punishment.
Adopted into God's forever family with a new name and identity.

When we fail as believers we are still alive in Christ:
We are still facing God.
We are still Justified and Forgiven.
We are still members of God's family with His name and identity.

Our failures are opportunities for growth and healing. James Chapter 5 tells how we can deal with every issue and problems as a Christian. Most of the people that came to LifeWay were true believers who had suffered at the hands of others. As a result they often gave up on God and even more on themselves. The Shame caused by abuse often led them to think they were useless so we always trained them with the skills of truth so they could practice Romans 12:1-2 that says "Do not be conformed to this world but be transformed by the renewing of your mind". This is how shame can be defeated and the brain can be healed from a lifetime of crazy, chaotic home life and toxic stress.

Shame always results in "Stinking Thinking" or shame filled, self-condemnation with the victim thinking what the abusers told them rather than what God says! We trained our Residents to reject the lies and refuse to give power to the abusers, including Satan. This can be, however, a lifelong struggle because "The world, the flesh and the devil conspire to destroy us."

Jesus was called The Great Physician because He came to "Heal the broken hearted and set the captives free." Victims of abuse are tempted to forget that the Great Physician is always on call to offer us grace and mercy in our time of need. When I visited the unit I regularly asked Residents, "How is the Lord treating you today?" they invariably answered, "Great. God is good all the time".

The Processes of Healing Toxic Stress and Trauma

Over the years we learned how to train people in the careful processes of ministry to traumatized persons. Great care must be taken to reduce the dangers of re-traumatizing the person that is suffering. An overly aggressive approach from overly concerned friends, Pastors, Evangelists and Christian leaders can leave the person worse rather than better. We tried to follow the passage that exhorts us to "Not allow anything to come from your mouth that fails to edify others". Ephesians 4:29

To edify is to build up. Prideful people, including Ministers, can come on so strongly that the Seeker is reminded of his or her past trauma and the second condition is worse than the first. This is one reason I resist trying to heal deep trauma from the platform or pulpit. It takes time, Love and patience. Think through these attached Steps of Ministry.

Think About This

Then I asked, "Are you treating yourself as good as the Lord treats you?" Quite often they acted shocked and said, "Oh no. That would be wrong. That would be prideful!" I would say, "Why is thinking like Jesus wrong?" We somehow think that offering grace and mercy and truth to ourselves is sinful! Friends, let us have the Mind of Christ! Shalom,

Dr. Gary Sweeten Lent, 2016

Resources
www.sweetenlife.com has many free and inexpensive books, video tapes, monographs, papers, etcetera, to guide your growth and healing. Sweeten, Gary R. Hope and Change for Humpty Dumpty, Power Christian Thinking, How to be Me in My Family Tree, Breaking Free, ETC.

On Confession, Forgiveness and Reconciliation
- John F. Hunt

Recently my wife Rosemarie and I had lunch with some very dear friends whom we do not see often enough. Both spoke of moving away from their Catholic faith, one to the Lutheran Church and the other to the Anglican Church, both religions very close to their Catholic roots. What I thought was interesting was the rejection of confession in their Catholic practice with no mention of its very real structured use and existence in their new practices. I remember many discussions with my classmates during parochial school recess about confession with most of them based on myths and exaggerations. In fact confession, forgiveness, reconciliation has always been hotly debated as it is for many so hard to accomplish. I mention this not to discuss how the process plays out in each religion but rather to show how it played out for Vicki. It wasn't easy as many Christians can attest but to emphasize that what is the hardest thing to do is often times the best thing to do.

To paraphrase Dr. Sweeten, discipline, conviction of sin and confession are not readily embraced by many and yet they are essential to the Christian life. These processes openly confront sin whereby we become free from the past and able to enjoy the fruits of righteousness. Vicki's life is filled with numerous episodes that show the power and benefits of confession and forgiveness. In her attempts to heal her relationships with her parents we see her gaining in strength of character and in the restoration of her spirit, soul and body. Her story also validates the old saying that the consequences of concealment greatly outweigh the consequences of confession.

When Vicki apologized to Lily and then later Ed for not being the daughter they wanted, these acts were very freeing events. She took the initiative to clean up her relationship with them as much as she could. Some counselors and friends would say it is wrong for a victim to apologize to those that have been cruel and uncaring. However, it gave Vicki strength and power over her hurts and showed her how strong she was in the Lord.

Then, she forgave them for the years of abuse! It is an amazing sense of freedom in having a Christ centered life. It is a life empowered by the grace of the Holy Spirit and tested by the challenges of everyday life just as Christ was tested. Those and other challenges taught her perseverance. In so doing she grew in maturity and a completeness so lacking in her abusers.

Many question why God can allow adverse things to happen to His believers, to good people. In giving her the grace to forgive He gave her the grace to grow as a person. It is in the difficulties of her life that she grew, that she was at her best. An analogy that I like says a river does not sing until it hits the rocks and other obstructions along its way.

In her growth Vicki is able to confess her faults and to forgive those around her of their wrongs. In attempting to heal herself she simultaneously ministered to others; the two are not separable.

Anam Cara is Gaelic for "soul friend." John O'Donohue defines soul friend as "one who awakens your life in order to free the wild possibilities within you." Although at first unwilling to share a room at LifeWay with a woman the same age as her mother Vicki became a soul friend to Ann and Ann to her. They bonded, they talked, they shared deep feelings and thoughts, and they opened up to each other in a way that they became healers to each other. When Ann knelt before Vicki and assumed the role of Lily, Vicki's mom, asking for forgiveness, it wasn't the professional staff or their pastors doing the healing but each other. So it is in confessing to God though a priest, it is not the priest but the act of confessing that creates the context for absolution. God who hears then confers the forgiveness that is so important for the person confessing to hear.

I remember from my bible history classes how the early Christians were Christ like to each other. They listened, they prayed, they confessed and they forgave as Christ had forgiven them. Christ, God made man, showed them how to live. The Holy Spirit gave them the grace and power to do as He preached – to love one another. Christ's command of going forth to spread the good news also included the charge to be priests to each other, to serve the need of others first least we lose our way. But to do that one must be clean in spirit. That would be easy if each person was perfect but no one is.

But there is a way to become Christ-like even in our imperfect selves: prayer, revealing our weaknesses and transgressions, love of others, forgiveness of others and mercy to others. The road to maturity, the road to healing is in being free of what brings us down. Love, mercy and grace build a highway of healing. It is freedom versus shame and unhealthy lifestyles. Prayer focused on forgiveness given to us in the words of the prayer – The Our Father.

When Lily repeatedly told Vicki she was neither good enough to be baptized nor would she ever be good enough to go to church she smothered Vicki in a blanket of shame. After years of such abuse the shame became who she thought she was; it became a core belief. It became her two edge sword; even though she saw that Christ offered something totally different and good, in her mind she wasn't good enough to go to church. Self-Shaming ideas said, "You are not good enough to get the help you know you need." It is a horrible double bind that keeps former victims with a mindset that keeps them victimizing themselves.

The more she came to know and trust Christ the more willing she was to accept His love, grace and her new identity. It is an identity that destroyed her shaming identity and gave her freedom to be the child of God. In the process she was able to confess her own weaknesses and to forgive those who hurt her. It begins with trust, trusting our new identity enough to be weak and vulnerable with others. Defensiveness can be overcome and boldness can grow. Before the healing can begin there has to be trust – authentic trust in the Lord, ourselves and in each other.

True healing only happens when trust can build a deep personal relationship with God and with those we interact, be they clinical professionals or those who are part of our dysfunctional family. Once authentic trust exists the hard work of forgiving, confessing and freeing oneself can begin. In freeing herself Vicki stopped what could have become another curse handed down to future generations.

Parents are instrumental in teaching their children basic core beliefs whether good or bad. Thus the core beliefs learned at the hands of abusive parents and others become the guiding principles handed down to their children and so the dysfunction continues into succeeding generations. The parents have sinned and the children are punished. But it doesn't have to go on forever. We can change that downward cycle of pain and dysfunction by allowing the reality of the new life fill us to the brim. Vicki proves it is possible to change our core beliefs for the better. She is in the process of restoring herself to what God intended her to be.

Along Vicki's journey people like Paula, Ann, Dr. Hanson, LifeWay, Connections, and Jim have been her Anam Cara, soul friends. In the process they have facilitated the healing of her soul, spirit and body. The harmonious relationship she is building with God and others is based on being free. Free from shame and guilt; free from an abused past life; free to think, feel and relate with more love, more power and more of Christ in her life. It is a harmony derived from learning to confess and reconcile with others; from forgiving those who hurt her and mistreated her. There is no need for bitterness; no desire for revenge; no need to confront the abusers. She has the freedom that only love, grace and mercy can bring. To paraphrase an old hymn: We are the Presence of God.

John F. Hunt 2016

Resources:
O'Donohue, John. Anam Cara: A Book of Celtic Wisdom. New York: Harper Perennial, 2004 Sweeten, Gary R, E.D. Breaking Free To Be All God Intended You To Be, Cincinnati: Sweeten Life Systems, 2013. Interview with Fr. Thomas Kreidler, Pastor, Immaculate Heart of Mary Catholic Parish, Cincinnati, OH

Kevin Lilly

On Making Good Connections
- Rebecca Born, MSW, LISW

"Let each become all he was created capable of being." Thomas Carlyle

The vision unfolded as Rachel and I pondered Jeremiah 1:5. I saw myself as a toddler, playing with Jesus. I was hiding among the folds of his robe, riding on his shoulders and playing with his beard. He didn't mind. As a matter of fact, he was taking great delight in the playfulness. I knew that the chuckle in his voice and the twinkle in his eye were because of his enjoyment of me.

As I watched, the toddler grew weary, and crawled into his arms and fell asleep. He gently put his hand on my head and my heart and I knew that he was imparting to me all that I needed to be me. Just like the scripture says. He set in place my character, my talents, my passions, my hopes, i.e. everything that I would need to be who he designed me to be on earth.

As I watched further, the picture changed to one with me on my bed, my parents standing at the foot. Their attitude reflected one of disapproval that they were disgusted and fed up with me. I watched as my mother said, "I don't know what to do with her. She asks too many questions, she does her own thing." My Dad agreed and shook his head.

As the vision ended, I understood deeper the need for restoration and the power found in authentic identity. You and I arrive to earth with the supernatural touch of God upon our identity. His handprint upon my being cannot be obliterated. It carries a supernatural power of His design. The world, however, is not always a loving safe place. Whether by sex abuse, emotional abuse, neglect or disregard, we are hurt. In order to get through it, we separate ourselves from the aspects of our identity that prove to be "unacceptable" and lose the knowledge of who we really are. When the time is right, we can go through a restoration process, clean off those improper labels, heal the hurt, and reconnect to our God created identity.

You are not what happened to you! Something happened *to* you and it shaped your thinking about yourself and the world around you. Those beliefs have directed your behaviors. Who you are, or your authentic identity, is not lost! The person you were created to be lies buried under the circumstances, lies and coping mechanisms developed from experiencing trauma. The journey of restoration entails identifying the falsehoods, shifting them and reconnecting to that authentic identity. Vicki's sharing of her journey reveals the challenges involved in this work and the possibilities of shifting to directing your life rather than being directed by the impact of trauma.

In Vicki's journey you can see how the impact of what she believed about herself and the atmosphere in which she lived had set her up for recreating generational patterns. With vulnerability she shares the dynamics of her previous marriages that reflect her beliefs about relationships and her value within them. By marrying men who were similar to her family dynamic of disregard for her and her needs, she was living out of trauma.

At the core of restoration work is the need for taking responsibility to identify the internalized messages of trauma and shift them. Restoration is achieved when the impact no longer dictates your thinking or behaviors. It is absolutely possible to deconstruct the impact. The following concepts are offered to help you utilize the core skills required for conquering the impact of sex abuse.

Recognize - We often live our lives on automatic pilot and need to begin to slow down enough to recognize internal messages. The things we tell ourselves to make sense of the world, or the things that have become beliefs as a result of your experiences, need to be recognized and interrupted.

When Vicki was able to identify and verbalize the words spoken over her and connect them to internal belief systems, she was utilizing this core skill. Once recognized, Vicki then could embark upon shifting them rather than being led by them.

Internalize –Internalize means to make something part of your own thinking. When you internalize the positive messages you have heard, you have internalized truth. Truth is defined as a thought or belief that moves you towards freedom, passion and destiny.

As Vicki embraces the love of God, her husband and friends and continues to be willing to internalize the positive words spoken over her, she will move beyond "always having to work on healing and believing good." Internalizing the truth of who she is as shown to her by loving and respectful people, now enables her to live out of purpose and destiny.

Exchange – You've heard that old saying, "Out with the old in with the new," that's making the exchange from the hurtful beliefs born of trauma to the truths that provide freedom! When you commit to exchanging the negative thoughts and beliefs with new ones, the direction of your life shifts.

When Vicki began to use boundaries, she shows evidence of having exchanged some of her thinking.
As she makes stands for herself and her boys, she is operating out of an exchanged sense of value.

Power of Agreement – You have the power to agree or disagree with what you've been told or believe about self. The beliefs born of trauma are lies about who you are. Using your power of agreement to disagree with the negativity and move towards agreeing with the positive truths creates space for experiencing and embracing your God given attributes.

The words spoken over Vicki such as, "ugliest kid ever," and "drama queen," and "not enough" created a deep wound that guided some behaviors that ultimately reinforced those statements. Without realizing it, she had created a power of agreement with them. The negative beliefs feel like truth and are experienced as real and natural. When Vicki began to grasp that she didn't have to agree with them, she became able to take the difficult steps of fighting for her rights and those of her children.

Her journey into a relationship with Beth and the opening of her shop, reflect how she is working to shift her power of agreement to connect with her authentic identity and live out of purpose.

Responsibility – The victim is never responsible for what happened, but ultimately is responsible to do the challenging work of conquering the impact and gaining control over the direction of her life. There comes a time when the victim must turn away from holding the trauma as a reason for dysfunction and hold herself responsible for shifting it. This level of taking responsibility is crucial to achieving total restoration to authentic identity. In this, the victim regains power!

When Vicki signed herself into Lifeway, she made the first step in taking responsibility for healing. Finding a therapist she can trust, and participating in groups provided the support and education needed to journey out of impact. Keep in mind, however, just showing up doesn't create the change. Taking responsibility to do the difficult work of shifting mindsets, behaviors and coping strategies is what creates restoration. Complete restoration is absolutely possible and requires the continual use of the core skills to produce the regeneration of beliefs about self.

Having read Vicki's journey, your heart may be ready to work on your own. To assist and encourage you, I offer for further exploration and assistance, additional information about the Restoration Paradigm.

The Restoration Paradigm provides a framework through which the journey to authentic identity and the power within can be attained. The framework consists of four restoration ranges:
Refugee: *"I don't understand the world and the world doesn't understand me."*
Overcoming: *"I am my story"*
Conquering: *"There is more to me than abuse."*
Identity: *"I am Me."*

Restoration: Focus on Self Awareness, not Memories
There is significant controversy surrounding therapeutic approaches utilized when working with the trauma of sex abuse. Traditional approaches focus on retrieving memories, releasing connected emotions and assimilating the trauma experience into one's reality (Herman 1992). It is our stance that memory retrieval alone does not provide for restoration and can prove to be more hurtful and disruptive than helpful. The Restoration Paradigm calls for a focus on assisting the sexually wounded in developing self-awareness rather than memory retrieval.

It is significant when someone reveals the secret of sex abuse. It is not in the revelation, however, that restoration happens. Secrets kept fester. Just as a splinter left in your finger will fester with an infection, so does the secret of sex abuse create an infection. The secret of sex abuse is the scar tissue that covers over the internal infection of the trauma. Simply stating the fact, "I was sexually abused," propels the speaker to a place of acknowledging that the secret is reality. That brings the victim a step towards relief, but does not produce restoration. It is in the unveiling of the secret that the source of the infection can be uncovered.

The source of the infection is not found in the details of the abuse itself. Simply retrieving the memory and sharing the details does not produce restoration. The source of the infection is actually found within the concepts and internal structures the wounded heart has spun in order to manage the trauma.

A child's mind is incapable of processing the traumatic reality he/she is experiencing. The mind is busy establishing mechanisms to understand what it can't comprehend. These mechanisms become the building blocks for future relationships with self, others and the world. These mechanisms and structures often operate below the surface without our awareness. When during the restoration process the focus becomes self-awareness, i.e. understanding what I'm thinking or believing about something, we gain the power to change the unhealthy internal structures. That is where life-giving restoration happens: From deep within. From the inside out.

Use of Language

Words shape the direction of our lives. The words spoken to us, around us and over us create pathways upon which our lives play out. Words can build up or tear down, set limits or promote freedom, encourage or discourage, bless or curse.

Understanding the importance of words and how they affect the victim of sex abuse is key to restoration. From the words the perpetrator uses during the crime, to the words the victim tells themselves and uses to describe their trauma; from the words the justice system uses to the words the mental health profession depends on; each set of words carries its own challenges. Each word spoken around the abuse carries an implication and an internalized meaning for the victim. Exploring and understanding the impact of the words the victim hears and uses is an important part of opening the pathway to freedom.

Reclaiming the word victim

I suspect you have noticed by now that we have reclaimed the word victim. I wonder if you have bristled some as you read it. Good! I want you to wrestle with these concepts. Victim is not a demeaning, nor a bad word. It is a more representative word of the reality experienced in sex abuse.

When we restore the definition of victim to its true definition *someone or something killed, destroyed, sacrificed, etc.; one who suffers a loss especially by being swindled* (Agnes, 2001), we see there is no weakness in it and that it correctly identifies the person battered by sex abuse. Something does get destroyed! No, more than something, *someone* gets destroyed! Value, personhood, beliefs, self-respect, deep core reservoirs of a person's strength and possibility are destroyed. Parts of the person, i.e., the capability to trust, to be intimate, or feel safe are sacrificed by the uncontrolled urges and needs of another. That is being a victim!

One of the reasons our culture has moved away from using the word victim is because we don't like the feeling the word gives us. Our society tends to hold a victim more responsible than a perpetrator. If your house is robbed, people ask if you locked the doors. If your purse is snatched, people question how you were holding it. If you are sexually abused, people ask why you went into that room. We first question the victim as if she did something wrong to create the scenario in which she was hurt. Seldom does the first response contain an outraged indictment that someone felt free to violate another's personal rights. The victim is blamed, made to feel "less than". So we don't want to be called a victim.

In the moment of victimization you are rendered powerless by someone else's actions. Power is highly esteemed in our culture, and we look less favorably on those without power. In the eyes of our culture being a victim means you did something wrong; you lost your power. The fact that as a victim you were powerless becomes unacceptable because power is so highly valued.

There is no inherent weakness in being a victim – things happen to us that are out of our control. Being a victim has become a derogatory mark upon one's personhood rather than the damaging event that it is. This indictment is wrong. There is no shame in being a victim. Shame says I need to feel bad because I did something wrong. A victim of sex abuse is not the one who did something wrong. The victim is never the one at fault!

When we fail to identify the person as a victim, we nullify their reality, congratulating them that they made it through, as we expect them to ignore the impact of the crime. On the outside they adopt the identity of survivor, meaning "I'm OK," while on the inside all they know is fear, uncertainty, intense pain, and loss of personal identity.

It is no wonder the victim of sex abuse hears, "put it behind you," "why are you still thinking about that," for as a culture we have told them by denying their victimhood that it IS over. We have told them in the use of our language that it IS all better – you survived! It is as if we hand them a badge we expect them to wear – a badge that says, "denial." This is wrong and destructive, and perpetuates and prolongs the damage of abuse.

Saying, "I'm a survivor" is *not* more empowering than saying, "I'm a victim". Victims have more power to get freedom than survivors do because victims remain in touch with the reality of the trauma impact. When the victim quickly becomes a survivor and jumps from the point of impact directly to claiming the status of being a survivor, they jump over a whole set of emotions, needs, thought processes, and confusion. When not connected to the reality of the emotions and belief systems, one cannot heal them. One can't fix what they don't know is broken. One can't become a survivor without knowing what they survived. Just because the event is over and that person is alive does not mean they know what they have overcome.

The use of "I am"

The use of the words, "I am," speaks of identity or parts of being. When we follow those words with a description of something we have come through (example: I am a cancer survivor), we link our identity with a situation or label and not aspects of who we are. This denies our identity and negates the internal resources that were utilized to bring us through that situation. It leaves us connected to the disease or abuse, and not connected to ourselves. Someone who overcame cancer utilized such internal things as will, faith, and strength; those assets should be highlighted. "My strength of will defeated cancer," is so much more empowering than, "I'm a cancer survivor". When we link "I am" to internal strengths and not the disease, we claim and develop the fullness of us. We don't allow the situation to describe us.

The use of the phrase, "I am an alcoholic," or "I am a survivor of sex abuse," teaches us and the world that we *are* that behavior or that trauma. It becomes a prison sentence with no hope of freedom from the problem. Even if we accept the idea that alcoholism or addictions are diseases, our language when speaking of them does not sound as if we believe they are diseases. By contrast, we don't say, "I'm a liver disease," or "I'm a high blood pressure". With those diseases we separate our identity from the illness. We say, "I have high blood pressure." There is an understanding through the language we use that I "have" something that is affecting me, but *it* isn't me. When we "have" something there is a sense of ownership but an acceptance that we have the ability to either keep it or release it. There is a sense of empowerment knowing we have the possibility of conquering the disease and move into life a more developed person.

Even beyond the identity issue we see in the use of "I am," the person traumatized by sex abuse has an additional struggle with the word survivor. Culturally, we have decided that it is acceptable to be a survivor of some things more than others. When someone says, "I'm a cancer survivor" or, "I'm a survivor of a war crime," we offer sympathy and congratulations. In those cases, it is culturally acceptable to "be" that. We celebrate that they have overcome the possibility of a death sentence. However, when someone says "I am a survivor of sex abuse," we offer silence and suspicion. We do not celebrate anything. As a culture we are so steeped in denial and an aversion to knowing about sex abuse that we demean and silence the victim.

Additionally, one cannot say they are a "survivor" of sex abuse until they have conquered the impact of the abuse. Having lived through the trauma doesn't qualify one as having survived. Because the real damage of sex abuse is in the hidden messages and beliefs of the victim, until those are changed, she hasn't survived.

The restoration paradigm changes the descriptive language we use around the issue of sex abuse. It separates the description of process from the identity of the person. Someone is not a survivor, but rather a *person* who survived, making her strengths her identity rather than the trauma. The restoration paradigm challenges any statement that begins with "I am" and verbally connects the victim to an aspect of abuse. The new language approach requests that the victim not possess the abuse.

Some common statements that a trauma victim might use with an "I am":

"I am damaged goods."

This statement dehumanizes and objectifies the person. Damaged goods are objects; things received at a loading dock with the package broken. Inherent in the statement is the belief that my only value lies in what I can do for you and I'm unacceptable as a result of trauma. Feel the difference when someone learns to say, "I was damaged by sex abuse." It names the source of the problem, separates it from identity, and allows for movement away from the damage.

"I am bad."

This statement reflects the victim trying to come to terms with what has happened to her. She is attempting to put things in order, to explain why she was sexually abused. This statement can be:

1. *A way to feel powerful* - Saying "I am bad" is a form of dissociation that distances the victim from the reality of her situation. In a strange way, "I am bad" helps the child experiencing trauma to feel powerful. If she is the bad one, then the people around her aren't and she is not trapped in an unsafe world. She is the problem and therefore, she has the power to correct it. If she allows herself to know that she *isn't* bad, and it *is* the people around her that are bad, then her world is not a safe place and she is powerless to change it.

2. *A stronghold* that keeps someone from moving forward in restoration. A stronghold is a fortified city; something that is staked down and immovable. Once turned into a stronghold, the belief is very difficult to change. Most victims of sexual abuse will live believing they are bad. Most of their interactions with themselves and others are based on that deep belief. The victim, who has turned this belief into a stronghold, will be uncomfortable in healthy relationships, new positive self-images, and receiving honor and respect. She is usually not willing to make the exchange in her belief system.

The victim whose message of "I am bad" has turned into a stronghold, will find it difficult, if not impossible, to try to treat herself with respect. Her first and foremost thought is always, "I am bad and nothing can change that". She can see that others in her situation are not bad, but cannot put herself into ANY category that declares that she is not bad. This belief becomes as real to her as her name.

The stronghold can become so powerful that the victim has made it her mantra. It is the response to everything positive spoken to her. There is no room to explore the possibility that she is not inherently bad. Sometimes there may be no real desire to explore that possibility. The victim, for as much pain as she is in, will not allow positive messages to penetrate her mantra that she is bad. She will not allow new teachings, new truths, new ideas to influence how she will set safe boundaries, how she will use self-respect to protect herself, or how she will be restored to all that she was created to be. Nothing compares to her insistence that she is bad.

The victim who carries "I am bad" as a stronghold, may put herself in a position to try new positive experiences. However, as she experiences them, they do not seem to have the power to help her re-write her belief that she is bad. Rather, they typically solidify her "I am bad" belief. The new positive experiences seem to serve as a reminder of how bad she believes herself to be. They cannot penetrate through to help her see herself in a more realistic light. The discrepancy between what she believes and what she is being told creates an internal conflict. Because she cannot live with such an internal conflict, she will often sabotage new truths.

In contrast if "I am bad" is not a stronghold, the victim is able to build positive experiences and messages based on new truths she is learning, and she becomes more and more aware that she really is not bad. She begins to make positive adjustments in her relationships and attitudes towards self. She continues to awaken to the realization that she needs to create healthier dynamics in her relationships. She may now have the freedom to experience a new found anger not only at what she experienced in the abuse, but also in what she may be experiencing in her current relationships.

"I am powerless."

The difference between recovery and restoration is found in the key use of the term powerless. In the recovery paradigm you remain powerless and captive by the disease or addiction. In restoration you make the shift to understand that for a time the trauma has rendered you powerless to experience life as you wish to but you are not powerless to conquer it. You regain the power and restore your innate strengths to live in your identity as a whole, powerful person. The correct phrase is, "I was powerless at the moment of trauma".

The use of "my"

The word "mine" is central to a two year old's world. He is distinguishing where he fits, where he belongs and what belongs to him. He knows that if he claims the ball as *mine*, the little girl trying to take away the ball will think twice!

The use of the word "my" denotes ownership. It says that this object, feeling or place belongs to me and I want it. The use of the word creates a picture of embracing, of keeping close to you, of holding on to something.

Every time the victim of sex abuse says, "my abuse" or "my perpetrator" or "my triggers," a sense of ownership is set up inside and around her. It makes it more difficult to put "it" away; to depart from and walk away. Feel the difference in the power of the words if you say "the abuse" rather than "my abuse"; "the perpetrator" rather than "my perpetrator". When you use the word "the," it distances the object from you, creating a space within which to explore if you want to keep it or not.

Get started today

Remember, you are not what happened to you! Trauma has shaped your view of the world. Your innate qualities coupled with a fighting spirit can reverse that impact. Your personal restoration journey can start today. Draw from Vicki's experience, utilize these core thoughts from the Restoration Paradigm and go for it!

Resources:

Born MSW, LISW, Rebecca: & Davis, MS, CFLE, Rachel. *Beyond Recovery To Restoration, Working With the Trauma of Sex Abuse,* Cincinnati; Thumbprint Publishing, 2009.

Born MSW, LISW, Rebecca: & Davis, MS, CFLE, Rachel. *Beyond Recovery To Restoration, Working With the Trauma of Sex Abuse -* The Workbook, Cincinnati; Thumbprint Publishing, 2010

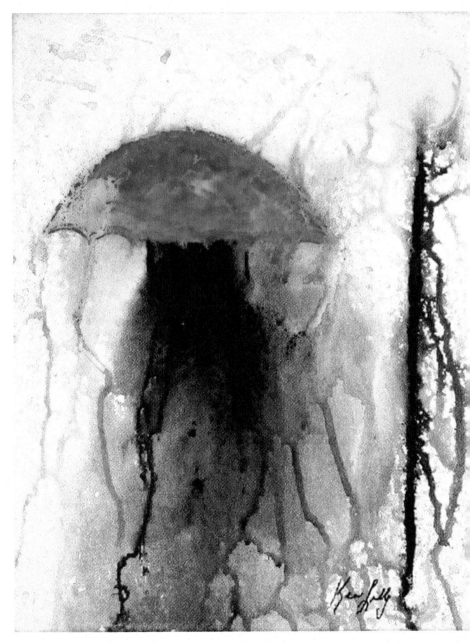

Kevin Lilly

On Family Dysfunction – John F. Hunt

As we were completing *Loving Me* crisis struck or as Vicki has said so often the devil attempted to stop this book. Both of Vicki's sons expressed their resentment and disapproval of Vicki for writing *Loving Me*. To them, "in speaking for the family," the book covered old news best left unsaid and the greater need was to protect the family. They came to this decision having not read the drafts that Vicki had sent them, early on, hoping to gain their loving support and approval. Additionally, they have promised not to buy, not to read and not to support this book which is their right to so choose. Additionally they have asked that their names and pictures be removed. All of their requests are within their rights to privacy and are acknowledged here as having been fulfilled.

From the Bible to Tolstoy to Conroy great authors have tried to show the dysfunctionality of families. Pat Conroy in his last book, The Death of Santini wrote that all families are dysfunctional. The challenge for every writer is that there is no one model of dysfunctionality; each family is different and thus travels its own path into this inferno called dysfunction. This reality crosses all borders: income, religion, philosophy, geography, race, culture, politics and lifestyle. In exposing the dysfunctionality and the reactionary argument that "the family needs to be protected" the question many writers face becomes "What *family* is there to protect?" What good is accomplished when the truth is hidden? If we do not learn from others will we always be condemned to repeat it? Will the victims always be victims? Does it matter? The ramifications of what the family hides are always greater, more severe and more painful than the ramifications of what is revealed.

One person thinks it matters. Danielle, Vicki & Jim's eighteen year old daughter, thought it was important enough to pen a response to her siblings. It is a response that I will excerpt here as it shows a writing ability well beyond her years, an incredible moral conviction and a steadfast love of the greater good. Here are three parts of this letter I wish to share.

With regards the old news and protect the family assertions:
...as we have established our mother, (the person that gave you life, the person who is still TO THIS DAY paying off YOUR student loans, the person who would do ANYTHING for you) was RAPED, BEATEN, ABUSED, NEGLECTED, INSULTED AND SHAMED BY HER FAMILY. News flash, darling: She wasn't the one who damaged those precious "family relationships"

Actually, look at the facts and she has tried NUMEROUS times to repair these relationships that OTHERS broke. She constantly tries to communicate and bond with members of her family, often ending in horribly abusive results. She asks for prayers and receives verbal abuse, insults, and doubts. They ask for prayers and she prays her heart out. She loves her family and wants them to love her despite all the hell they have put her through. It seems ridiculous that her own son, one of her closest family members, would also verbally abuse and throw blatant lies at her. She has come to you in her most broken state, shown you all her wounds, shown you the scars that litter her spirit, wanting little more than support for having written an ENTIRE BOOK and you have the nerve to accuse her of attention seeking?

How many times did you go to her with bloody knees and ask for help, to have her bandage your skin and kiss your wounds? How would you have felt if she had jammed her fingers knuckle deep into your flesh, essentially what you have done to her?

With regards the claim that the book was written to benefit a few over the family:

Those "few" you speak of are actually 17.7 million American rape victims, 3.6 million victims of child abuse, 715,000 American incest victims, and 350 million people suffering from depression.

If you think that mom's books won't touch any of those people, you are dead wrong. Saturday, I was at mom's store working when a woman from church (not a "close" friend of mom's, but an acquaintance) came into the store, almost with tears in her eyes and said how touched she was by mom's book, and how inspired she was. Our mother wrote something that touched someone's soul in a positive, healing way, which is more than any of us can say. She not only survived abuse, but she overcame it. She conquered it. She is teaching others to conquer it.

Having used logic Danielle then turns to a spiritual presentation:
Matthew 5:16 *In the same way, let your light shine before others, so that they may see your good works and give glory to your Father who is in heaven.*

Mother is offering her story as a beacon of hope for the hopeless. She is not doing it to glorify herself but to glorify God. If you truly read her book then you would understand that.

Romans 12:6-7 *"We have different gifts, according to the grace given to each of us. If your gift is prophesying, then prophesy in accordance with your faith; if it is serving, then serve; if it is teaching, then teach;" Mother's gift is her ability to express herself through words. Her gift is to act as a screen on which God may project his awesome healing power. By writing this book she is using the gift he has given her. She is doing his work.*

Ephesians 4:29 *Let no corrupting talk come out of your mouths, but only such as is good for building up, as fits the occasion, that it* *may give grace to those who hear. Mother's book is not about insult-ing people, it is about building up victims into places of healing with the help of God. She is a vessel of God's grace.*

Romans 12:14 Bless those who persecute you; bless and do not curse them. Never once does mother curse or insult her abusers. She hopes that they find healing, just as she has. It would fill her with intense joy to see her family healed and whole, she does not seek punishment for the guilty, otherwise she might have sued someone, or publicly slandered them. Even in her 100% TRUE book she is choosing to change the names of her abusers so that they will not be persecuted.

Psalm 118:17 I shall not die, but I shall live, and recount the deeds of the LORD. Our mother has been suicidal several times in her life. She has been on the verge of death from illness several times in her life. But she has survived, and she has given all the glory to God, her savior. Now she has written a book to honor all the mira-cles he has performed in her life.

///TO ADDRESS YOUR LATEST INSULT IN WHICH YOU ASK "WELL WHAT DOES _____(Name a family member)___ THINK ABOUT THE BOOK?"/// What does Gus think about the book?

Gee I don't know. I wonder what the man that brought our mother spiritual and emotional abuse, long lasting trauma, and nightmares to this very day, fear, and disdain from her own children thinks about mom writing a book about her healing? I never thought to ask him.

Because it's not his story.

What does Sissy think about the book?

Gee I don't know. I wonder what the woman so crippled from her own emotional trauma that she can barely even leave her house out of fear thinks about mom writing a book about her healing and how others may be healed through the grace of an almighty heavenly Father? I never thought to ask her. Because it's not her story.

What do Abe and Jack think about the book?

Gee I don't know. I wonder what the boys that owe her their life, that she worked tooth and nail to defend and care for, that she bought stupid Air Jordan's for when she didn't have money to eat on, who she supported through everything, who she loves more than herself, who she prays for and thanks God for everyday, who she would drop everything and run to RIGHT NOW, despite all the insults they have thrown at her would think about mom writing a book about God's wonderful mercy and the splendid life he has given her now? I never thought to ask them. Because it's not their story.

What does Beth think about the book?

Gee I don't know. I wonder what the child that she bore throughout months of shame and ridicule, the child that she chose to give away, the child she chose to save from the hellhole of a family she'd been raised in, the child that was given a chance at normalcy that she never had thinks about mom writing a book about love and redemption, forgiveness and healing? I never thought to ask her. Because it's not her story.

What does Amy think about the book?

Gee I don't know. I wonder what the woman who called my mother crying that her immature husband wanted to get a divorce and leave her alone with a one month old baby, only to have our mother DROP EVERYTHING, spend money she can't afford, fly across the country, and fight with her thinks of our mom, the woman that practically saved her marriage, thinks of mom writing a book on the importance of positive relationships, not only with people but with God above? I never thought to ask her. Because it's not her story.

The point is you can fill the blank with whatever name you want and it is still the same answer. What you, I, she, he, or they think is completely and utterly irrelevant. What mom thinks about the book is completely and utterly irrelevant. Because it's not her story.

It's God's story. It's His story of the unbelievable miracles He can and will perform for those He loves. It's His story of His strength. It's His story of His power. It's His story (of) His triumph over all the demons of hell.

It's God's story. So if you have a problem with it:

Take it up with HIM

How has Vicki taken this? It has been a very difficult time, hours of tears. Losing what she had hoped to be her sons' support has been emotionally draining. In Vicki's family there are, as Pat Conroy wrote, no crimes beyond forgiveness? But then she wrote:

Last night I had a dream and I would like to share it with you: I was at a theatre getting ready to perform. The audience was loud and rude. They were talking and laughing and making noises. The lights dimmed and it was my turn to perform, but the audience didn't quiet any. I dove into a beautiful pool of water and lights glistened and somehow I danced upon the water and there was beauty all around me.

At the end of my performance I once again dove down into the water and then shot out on a rainbow of bright lights. The audience was silent. All eyes were on me and then the room filled with applause. Then someone made an announcement. My performance had raised one million dollars for a charity and the people of this charity were rescued and safe. It was the highest amount ever raised in one performance for any charity. Then I woke up.

I laid in bed thinking about that dream for a long time afterwards unable to go back to sleep. I can't make my sons or anyone read the book, but for those who do read it.......God has promised hope. Hope for those who are currently a victim and hope for those who are currently in the field to help the victims. Hope is needed. I have no doubt this dream was God's way of encouraging me to go on. His hand is on this book.

Resources:

Conroy, Pat, The Death of Santini, New York: Nan A. Talese / Doubleday, 2013
Tolstoy, Leo, Anna Karenina, New York: Penguin Books, 2000

Kevin Lilly

LOVING ME

On Hope – Vicki Watkins

Writing any book can be challenging; writing this book about brokenness, incest, statutory rape, abuse, neglect, and serious illnesses was beyond challenging. It was gut wrenching!

Why write it you may ask? The answer can be said in one word: hope.

People in this world need hope. All of us come upon seasons of great suffering and loss. Without hope we will not survive. Without hope we will not heal. Without hope we will not succeed.

Hope can come in many fashions and shapes. Hope can enter the rooms of our hearts dressed in the royalty of our King's love. Or dance in on the arms of earthly angels. Hope can beat down the barriers of our heart and march in as a mighty army of faith. Hope can wait in the shadows of our heart and then suddenly appear as a kind word or hug. Yes, hope has many forms, it can even appear in the form of a book, held in the hands of a reader who needs hope, and enter the heart in just the right words at just the right moment.

My sons are precious to me. I am quite proud of the fine young men they have become, but because the hurt they went through, they just aren't there yet. Simply meaning they love me, but they don't want to share my hope with me right now.

They have their own journey to healing, we all do. I was very hurt when they ask for their names to be changed and their pictures to be removed. I cried a thousand tears. I took it as a personal attack on my being. But because of the rejection I so often suffered in the past I confused their non-understanding as rejection.

Now after I have had time to reflect, pray, cry and review all that I have learned, I know what it really is.......they are just not ready to cross the bridge into my hope with me. Not yet. Maybe someday. Maybe first they have to cross their own bridges. In the mean time I can only hope, and that is quite a big step for me.

Vicki Watkins 2016

Appendix

Vicki,

Your story is one for the nations to celebrate.
Now you don't have to look back.
Keep going under the stars of Christ.

Gary Sweeten
A Note June 2016

People in Vicki's Life

Parents, Aunts Uncles

Ed	Father
Lily	Mother
Oscar	Lily's Lover
Uncle B	Ed's brother
Uncle C	Ed's brother
Aunt Jennie	Ed's Sister
Barb	Ed's Second wife
Aunt Birdie	Lily's sister

Brothers, Sisters, Spouses

Kent	Brother (14-1/2 years older)
Joy	Wife #1
Teri	Wife #2
Reba	Wife #3
Sissy	Sister (13-1/2 years older)
Fred	Husband
Joe	Brother (5 years younger)
Chuck	Step-brother (Ed & Barb)

Men in Her Life

Ted	Predator #1 the Rapist & Beth's father
Steve	Husband #1 (no children)
Gary	Predator #2
Tony	Abe's father
Ryan	Husband #2
	Gus Husband #3 & Jack's father
	Tami Gus' Wife
	Jim Husband #4 & Danielle's father

Children, Spouses, Grandchild

Beth	Daughter, given to adoption
Abe	Son
Amy	Wife
Alex	Vicki's first grandson
Jack	Son
Danielle	Daughter

Cousins

Linda	Cousin (owner of KY porch)
Eddie	Cousin (owner of KY porch)
Ray	Cousin

Friends, Acquaintances, Counselors

Ann	Mother-like friend
Betty	Paula's mother
Brian	Older neighborhood boy
Cindy	Party girl
Count	Kent's buddy, visited Lily
Dr. Hanson	directed her to LifeWay
Linda M	supported Vicki
Paula	Lifelong friend
Phyllis	Neighbor & friend
Rachel	Connections, A Safe Place
Rebecca	Connections, A Safe Place
RuthAnn	Moms-in Touch
Sandy	Pastoral Counseling
Trish	Friend who provided shelter
Miss Wantuck	School teacher
Willie	Friend

Ed's letter to Lily while at Rollman Psychiatric Hospital.

Sunday Morning

Just a few lines to say hello Hope every one is ok hows the children I sure dont feel so good this place is like a rest home but it is cold out side I dont know how long I will stay in here till they let Me out for sure No one can get out on their own Please write to Me for it sure is a sad Place Sure would like to see the children I dont know what happened when I was there what ever did I am Very sorry I still wasnt at My self when they brought Me here Friday do you know where Bee + boys got hurt on

2

nat if this place dont make
people stop limping there
is some thing elel wrong
well I never was much a
writer I dont know what
I am attout to haue here
yet there will be a social
worker around Monday I
think did the Papers
from Kirk & Blune come
they need to be filled out
you can come see Me
if you wont to if not
write to Me let Me know
Hau the Children are

By now Ed

Ramans Hospital
3009 Burnette aue
Cinti   ahio

Lily Claims Draft Exemption For Oldest Son

Cincinnati, Ohio

Date- Nov. 18, 1967

State of Ohio
County - Hamilton
ss

This is to certify that my son [   ]
[   ] was the only means of support for me
his mother, Lily [   ] also his brother
[   ] age 2 years and his sister Vicki age
6 years for the year of 1966, except the assistance that I received from welfare which
proof is enclosed.

Lily R.[   ]

Lily [   ]

Sworn to before me this
18 day of December 1967,

Dorothy C. Butler
Notary Public

Vicki Surrenders First Child

Form Prescribed by
Department of Public Welfare
State of Ohio

PERMANENT SURRENDER OF CHILD

CWM 302 (Rev. 8/72)

TO COMPLY WITH SEC. 5103.15, SEC. 5103.16, AND SEC. 5153.16 (B) REVISED CODE OF OHIO

The undersigned ....**Vicki** [____]..
 ((*Name of parents, father, mother or guardian*)*

residing at ......**3735 Regent Avenue**........**Cincinnati**...............**Hamilton**....................
 (*Street-R.F.D*) (*City*) (*County*)

.....**Ohio**....................................... the ....**mother**...
 (*State*) (*Parents, father, mother or guardian*)

of ...**Female Infant** [____]........................... born the .....**1st**...... day of ...**June**......................, 19 **76**
 (*Name of Child*)

in ....**Cincinnati**..................**Hamilton**................**Ohio**...
 (*City*) (*County*) (*State*)

desires that said child be received by ..**The Children's Home of Cincinnati, Ohio**..........................
 (*Name of certified institution or organization, board or department*)

being unable to care for said child for the following reasons: ..**The undersigned is unmarried on the date hereof**
 (*Give detailed reasons why cannot care for child*)

...**and is unable to care for said child for social and economic reasons.**..................................

....

....

....

therefore does hereby surrender and entrust to the managing officers of said institution, organization, board, or department, the permanent guardianship of said child.

It is agreed that such managing officers shall have the sole and exclusive guardianship of said child and the right to place him/her in a foster home and to consent in court to his/her adoption, as provided in Section 3107.01 and 3107.06 of the Revised Code of Ohio.

It is further agreed that the undersigned will abide by the rules and regulations of the certified institution or organization, board or department, not to communicate with said child, or induce him/her to leave the institution or family with whom he/she might be placed, and to sever all connections with said child unless other arrangements are made by the certified institution or organization, board or department because of exceptional circumstances.

Witness my hand this ....**7th**........day of......**June**..............., 19 **76**

Witnessed by :

....

....
 (*Father*)**

 † *Vicki* [____]
 (*Mother*)**

 ....
 (*Guardian*)

*When the Mother and Father are living every reasonable effort should be made to obtain signatures of both.
**If only one parent signs explain legal basis.

THE STATE OF OHIO)
) ss:
Hamilton............... COUNTY)

Vicki [____].. being duly sworn, says she has voluntarily

signed the foregoing permanent surrender, the same having been carefully read and explained, and that statements there in are true to the best of her knowledge.

 ....
 † *Vicki* [____]

Sworn to before me and signed in my presence this ..**7th**......day of....**June**......,19 **76**

VINCENT T. WOERMANN
Notary ... ... Hamilton County, Ohio
My Commission Expires ... 15, 1980
 (OVER)

 ......**Juanita J. Wormann**......
 Notary Public in and for **Hamilton** County, State
 of Ohio

We, the undersigned Trustees (or duly appointed Admission Committee) of the ....

....
(Name and address of certified institution or organization, board, or department)

after careful and impartial consideration of all available facts, believe that ....
(Name of child)

is a suitable child to be received by ....
(Name of certified institution or organization, board, or department)

by reason of the fact that ....
(State circumstances causing dependency)

....

We, therefore, authorize and direct ....
(Name of superintendent-director-executive secretary)

to receive such child.

```
        (  ..........................................        ..........................................
        (
SIGNED: (  ..........................................        ..........................................
        (
        (  ..........................................        ..........................................
                                                                        (Date)
```

If the executive of the organization or institution has been authorized to accept the guardianship and custody of children by surrender, complete the following instead of above.

Cincinnati, Ohio

I, Norman W. Paget, Executive Director of The Children's Home of / ....being duly authorized to
(Name of executive of certified institution or organization, board or department)

accept the guardianship and custody of children by surrender do hereby accept full guardianship and custody of Female

Infant R▮▮▮▮ from mother, Vicki N▮▮▮▮
(Relationship and name of person executing surrender)

Witnessed by: Sadie Segal

Edna ▮▮▮▮▮▮ EXECUTIVE DIRECTOR
The Children's Home of Cincinnati, Ohio

....

STATE OF OHIO)
Hamilton ....COUNTY) ss:
)

Norman W. Paget ....being duly sworn says that he has carefully read the foregoing statements and that they are true
to the best of his knowledge.

Sworn to before me and signed in my presence this 7th day of June 19 76

Vincentia T. Woermann
(Notary Public)

*With consent of Juvenile Court
Per:

....   Date ....
(Judge of Juvenile court)

*Does not apply in surrenders to certified private agencies or institutions.

To be signed in duplicate, one copy to be retained by parent or guardian, one by the agency.

PART THREE   283

2-14-09

Dear Vicki

I'm not good about picking up cards or little things to sent to people I love + care about, like you are. So I'll tell you how I feel. When you where little + saying "me to" everytime I moved I loved it, I wanted someone I could hold + love + be close to. I thought I'd always be there for you, but life was to hard to stay around.

Never once did I stop loveing you, I just went on with my life in my own little world at that time I was happy + at peace, far away from all the pain it home.

God has brought us close to each other now because he knows, nomatter what we do, we will always except each other and love each other. My ways are different then yours, and that is what

II

makes us so close. You don't
make fun of me, your always building
me up & makeing me fell like
I'm somebody.
    We have both had alot of
pain in our life's, but to geather
we can let go' of our bogage
& think good thoughts everytime
we are togeather.
        I do love you very much,
and God has blessed me with
a wondaful sister.
        Thank you for all
the wondaful things you do.
        You will always be my
little "me too"

                Love
                     us

Vicki's Letter to Lily

9/13/12

Dear Mom,

Hospice has been called in and I know that your time here on earth is getting shorter.

You have been the dominate factor in this family for so long. I have seen the good of that and the bad.

When we get to heaven it says there will be no more pain, no tears. I know that you will be completely healed and whole and I thank God for that.

Most of the time you and I have sat on different sides of the fences, but I always knew I could put my hand through that fence and you were there, not too far away.

I think we both made mistakes and I think we

both tried to love each
other the best of our
ability. I hope you know
that I hope you know
that I really did try to
have a healthy relationship
with you and you meant
so much to me, that I
continued to try until
the day you die.

I can't go back there, I
can't revisiting the past and
I can't be around people
who continue to want to
take me there. I think
you will understand that
once you get to heaven and
see peace.

I love you mom and I will
miss you. I will miss all
the good memories I have of
us and I will forget all
the not so good. Be in
peace and know that God
will never leave or forsake

us. He is big enough to carry us, we will be fine. I love you mom. We both know the truth. I've been accused of not speaking the truth, but when I did noone wanted to accept it.

I think you need to hear from me, if not now certainly when you get to heaven. I forgive you mom and I hope you forgive me for any pain I ever caused you. I know you could never say you were sorry to me here on earth. It just wasn't in you, I don't know why, but I understand. Some people can't, just as long as things are taken care of between you and God that is what counts.

Remember when I sat in your dining room years ago and tried to talk to you?

I did tell you I was sorry, but the conversation was one sided. You couldn't talk to me or admitt to anything. Thats OK. Its long over and I have moved on and determined to keep going forward. There is a million questions that you will never answer, a million questions of why, but now I realize that its not as important as I once thought it was. So this is goodbye. I love you. I'll keep all the good memories locked in my heart forever. I'm locking up the bad ones and giving them to God. Its time we both let them go.

Love,
Vicki

Connections Worksheet #1

Breakthrough what is wrong

A victim of sex abuse will often rely on the things they were taught that is wrong with them rather than the things that are right with them Quote:

Even as a victim goes through the restoration journey, she will often cling more tightly to the things 'that are wrong as opposed to the things that are right.

In the beginning of her journey there is a reason she does this. It is because she is just becoming aware that her thoughts, behaviors, choices have been impacted by the abuse and perhaps for the first time she is hearing and learning about all the things that are positive, right, and special about her. Then the goal becomes getting her to make the exchanges that will help her live out of what is right rather than the negative.

If the victim is not careful she is in danger of grasping tightly to the wrong/negative things more tightly than she does the positive and right things about her. Because she has been heard, learned new possibilities but continues to live out of wrong, she may have crossed the line from the reasons she lives out of the negative into making excuses to not make the exchanges.

What is the difference?:

- Reason - a cause or an explanation. Reasons let us know where things originated, the are the why.
- Excuse - attempt to lesson the blame. Excuses can be overcome and removed, It takes willingness and self confrontation. And letting go of resistance in making the necessary exchanges.

Common reasons:

⇒ Abuse

⇒ Just learning trust

⇒ Has never been taught anything positive about self

⇒ Unstable early home life

⇒ Initial fear of believing something new

⇒ Initial fear of the unknown

Common Excuses:

⇒ Fear

⇒ Feelings of guilt

⇒ Unwillingness

⇒ Comfortable with what it is doing for you (usually related to other's reactions of care)

⇒ Difficulty in taking responsibility for what needs to be done to heal

LOVING ME

Connections Worksheet #2

As you address the excuses portion of this worksheet, remember we are not looking for the reasons or the things that happened to you, we are looking for the resistance inside you that hinders your making the exchanges. Also be specific in completing this.

The REASON I don't live out of the positive parts of myself such as __any thing , everything believing in myself__ , is because My past experiences with living out of the positive parts of me caused __pain, heartache, abuse__ _____ and I was __hurt, crushed, assaulted__ .

The EXCUSES I tell myself and probably others that I can't let go of the negatives is because I don't want to push myself to __fail (I fear failure)__ _____ and let go of __fear (fear of failure)__ because I would rather _____ __feel safe__ _____

> "Too often we are ruled by everything that's wrong with us as opposed to everything that's right with us."
>
> ~ Nick Ortner

In the space below use words, concepts, thoughts, picture, etc to describe the battle of overcoming excuses that keep you grasping more tightly to what is wrong/negative about you than what is positive/right with you. The portrayal of resistance

Scrapbook

Ed & Lily

Wedding Day 1946

Ed, Lily & Vicki is

13 months old.

**Vicki, Ed, Lily,
and Sissy when
she scratched
herself out of
the picture.**

**Ed, with his mother holding
Vicki after brain surgery.**

Lily, Sissy, Kent, & Ed

Lily, Vicki, Oscar

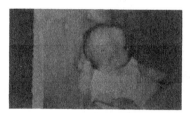

Vicki @ 15 mos with surgery scar

Vicki after syrgery

Sissy with Vicki 4 yrs

Vicki age 6

Wedding Day September 26, 1992
Jim , Vicki, with sons

Vicki & Anne
Mothers Day 2004

Vicki & Linda M.

Vicki & Paula
Those Reynolds Girls

Jim on Maine Trip 2015

Daniele 2015

Baby Alex

The Joy of Grandparenting

PART THREE

Bibliography

Literature

Born, Rebecca, MSW, LISW and Davis, Rachel, MS, CFLE, *Beyond Recovery To Restoration Working with the Trauma of Sex Abuse*, Cincinnati: Thumbprint Publishing, 2009

Born, Rebecca, MSW, LISW. and Davis, Rachel, MS.CFLE. Go *Beyond Recovery To Restoration Workbook*, Cincinnati: Thumbprint Publishing, 2010

Sweeten, Rev. Gary, E.D. and Griebling, Steve, M.S.; Hope and Change for Humpty Dumpty - Successful Steps to Healing, Growth & Discipleship, Cincinnati: Sweeten Life Systems, 2010

Townsend, J. T., *Queen City Notorious*, College Station, Texas: Virtualbookworm.com Publishing, 2014

Watkins, Vicki. *Against the Tide (A Book of Poetry)*, Denver, Outskirts Press, 2014

Women's Devotional Bible 2, New International Version

On-Line

Shepherd's Hill Journal December 2016, The Power of Gratitude

Illustrations

About the Authors

Vicki W. Watkins

Vicki Watkins lives with her husband Jim Watkins of 23 years in Cincinnati, Ohio. She is the published author of the inspirational poetry book, "Against the Tide" and owns "Under the Stars" Art Gallery/ Shoppe in Batavia, Ohio. Where she sells the beautiful creations of over 100 different artists and is blessed to be able to share their beauty with the world. Her favorite Bible verse is Philippians 4:13 "I can do all things through Christ which strengthens me" and one of her favorite sayings is "Pay more attention to your Creator than to your critics."

KEN,
IN SERVING OTHERS, WE PRAISE GOD.

[signature]
2016

John F. Hunt

John lives in Batavia, Ohio, with Rosemarie D'Occhio Hunt. They have been married for 44 years and have three children. When not spending time with their four grandchildren, John is the Executive Director of the Jason William Hunt Foundation. Named for their son the foundation provides scholarships for teens and young adults at-risk and in trouble to attend therapeutic wilderness expedition programs where they learn to believe in themselves. John is the published author of *Walking With Jason*.

CPSIA information can be obtained
at www.ICGtesting.com
Printed in the USA
LVOW05*0134021216

515373LV00011B/106/P

9 781478 780068